Early Hydraulic Civilization in Egypt

PREHISTORIC ARCHEOLOGY AND ECOLOGY

A Series Edited by Karl W. Butzer and Leslie G. Freeman

Karl W. Butzer

Early Hydraulic Civilization in Egypt

A Study in Cultural Ecology

The University of Chicago Press

Chicago and London

Karl Butzer is a professor in the Oriental Institute and in the departments of Anthropology and Geography at the University of Chicago. He is a member of Chicago's committees on African Studies, on Archaeological Studies, and on Evolutionary Biology. He also is North American editor of the *Journal of Archaeological Science*, editor of the Prehistoric Archeology and Ecology series, and the author of numerous publications, including *Environment and Archeology*, *Quaternary Stratigraphy and Climate in the Near East*, *Desert and River in Nubia*, *Geomorphology from the Earth*, and *Dimensions of Human Geography*.

The University of Chicago Press, Chicago 60637
The University of Chicago Press, Ltd., London

© 1976 by The University of Chicago
All rights reserved. Published 1976
Printed in the United States of America
80 79 78 77   98765432

Library of Congress Cataloging in Publication Data
Butzer, Karl W.
    Early hydraulic civilization in Egypt.

    (Prehistoric archeology and ecology)
    Bibliography: p.

    1. Egypt--Civilization--To 332 B. C. 2. Human
ecology--Egypt. 3. Irrigation--Egypt--History.
I. Title. II. Series.
DT61.B97   333.9'13'0932   75-36398
ISBN 0-226-08634-8
ISBN 0-226-08635-6 pbk.

For INA

CONTENTS

ILLUSTRATIONS

TABLES

FOREWORD

Early Hydraulic Civilization in Egypt is a fundamental contribution to knowledge of the cultural ecology of civilization
in the Nile Valley. While the book extends the temporal range
of publications scheduled for the Prehistoric Archeology and
Ecology series well into more recent millennia, the nature of
the problems Butzer treats and the perspective in which they are
seen are obviously as central to the series' purpose as works
dealing with early prehistory. In my opinion, this is the first
effective attempt to isolate, understand, and synthesize the
critical factors involved in the rise of an "irrigation civilization."

Butzer deals in depth with all the available data on changing environmental conditions, population and settlement density,
and technological factors and their probable effects on and
interaction with developing social and political organization.
The book shows how effective the integration of information from
historical documents into multidisciplinary research may be.
Incidentally, Butzer's analysis should convince historians and
prehistorians alike that the information they could derive from
techniques that each camp too frequently disdains as the province
of the benighted others is truly of vital importance to all who
study the history of early civilizations.

This book presents a fundamentally new view of "hydraulic
civilization" in the Nile Valley: a pragmatic view that I
believe is proving vastly more productive than traditional approaches to the material. Most important, Butzer shows us a
picture of emergent urban civilization that convincingly demon-
strates the gradual nature of that emergence and the thorough
interdependence of the relevant environmental, technological,

economic, ideological, and social factors involved. The view is in striking contrast to the position of those who tell us that civilization and urbanism appeared as a sudden consequence of new developments in ideology, politics, or social organization alone.

As co-editor, it gives me great pleasure to offer *Early Hydraulic Civilization in Egypt* as the third volume in the Prehistoric Archeology and Ecology Series.

LESLIE G. FREEMAN

PREFACE

The first domestication of plants and animals marked a turning point in prehistoric man-land interactions. Patterns of resource perception, subsistence, and adaptation that had served 100,000 generations of hunter-gatherers during the course of Pleistocene prehistory now rapidly became obsolete. As modes of food production were repeatedly improved, some regions saw the development of irrigation farming while others witnessed the evolution of urban institutions and the growth of cities. These steps toward intensive land use and high population densities have received considerable attention by anthropologists and social historians, in no small part because these phenomena are pertinent to interpretation of contemporary social landscapes.

On several floodplains of the Old World, the development of irrigation farming and urbanism appear to have gone hand in hand to produce a number of "hydraulic" civilizations. The term *hydraulic* refers to piped or channeled water and, to many, conveys an added flavor of engineering. In this sense, as applied to a floodplain society, it is largely synonomous with irrigation. But, mainly through the writings of Karl Wittfogel, *hydraulic* has attained the added connotation of those social and political processes leading to or culminating in a system of "Oriental despotism." Whatever one may think of Wittfogel's interpretations and generalizations, the basic fact remains that several of the earliest civilizations were identified with hydraulic systems conditioned to natural floodplains. There is here an unmistakable element of ecology, of a dynamic interface between environment, technology, and society. Yet ecological perspectives on the emergence of the great hydraulic civilizations have been crudely simplistic or otherwise ignored.

Preface

Irrigation, as a complexly structured agricultural and socio-economic system, develops through several adjustments, at least some of which are sequential. First, there is the generally new relationship of man to an environment now perceived as agricultural. Second, there is change within the structural properties of both the interpersonal and institutional relationships inherent to the society. Finally, there is the new man-land interrelationship that results from the interaction of the evolving social forms and the previous, agricultural man-land relationships. Only by understanding the mechanisms underlying these adjustments can the extent of change in man's interrelationship with his environment be properly understood.

A comprehensive, ecological approach to this fundamental problem of evolving land use and land ethic is clearly warranted. Such a theoretical framework can conveniently focus on three independent variables, on or through which the fourth variable is modeled. The independent variables are environment, technology, and population (in terms of demographic or cultural content or both). The dependent variable in this equation is social organization and differentiation, with factors such as trade, religion, and warfare functionally interwoven.

This study seeks to examine the emergence of a civilization in the Nile Valley that was ultimately based on irrigation farming. Unlike previous attempts, the approach is explicitly ecological. For this reason the temporal coordinates include ten millennia of prehistory and three of historical time. The methodology is necessarily interdisciplinary but, unlike most of my writings, it makes optimum use of the wealth of historical information provided by ancient Egypt. As a result, my primary focus is on the Pharaonic period.

In trying to achieve a degree of competence in utilizing so many categories of research, I was immeasurably aided by critical commentaries from and repeated discussions with Klaus Baer (Chicago). Charles Van Siclen and Edward Wente (Chicago) gave advice on source materials and chronological problems, as well as assistance in the transliteration of ancient Egyptian toponyms. A preliminary draft was presented at the International Egyptological Congress, Cairo, January 1975, and profited from conversations with George Cowgill (Brandeis), Barry Kemp (Cambridge), and Bruce Trigger (McGill). The next-to-last draft was critically read by Manfred Bietak (Austrian Archaeological Institute), Fekri Hassan

(Washington State), Kemp, and Trigger. Finally, I owe a debt to Daniel Bowman (Hamline) and John Van Allsburg (Michigan State) for stimulating discussions of some of the intellectual premises reflected herein. The illustrations were drawn with the usual care by Christopher Mueller-Wille (Chicago).

KARL W. BUTZER

INTRODUCTION

The late fourth millennium B.C. saw the emergence of one of
the earliest and most aesthetic of high civilizations in the Nile
Valley, and ever since Bonaparte's *savants* first surveyed its
antiquities (Herold 1962), Egypt has mesmerized scholars and a
large segment of the lay public. Archeology in Egypt was pace-
setting in the 1890s, as exemplified by Flinders Petrie's excavation methodology (Daniel 1967, pp. 232 ff.), while the prehistoric
surveys of Caton-Thompson and Gardner (1929, 1932) and of Sandford
and Arkell (1929, 1934, 1939) can now be viewed as milestones in
the development of interdisciplinary archeology. Yet a long era
of stagnation in archeological research and conceptualization
set in with the financial crisis of 1933, and, until very recently,
Egyptian archeology was largely preoccupied with art, architecture,
and pottery (for example, Baumgartel 1947-60, 1970). Even the
Nubian Monuments Campaign of the 1960s, which revolutionized
Paleolithic studies in Egypt (see Wendorf and Schild 1975; Butzer
1975b), contributed relatively little to a better understanding
of the late prehistoric record (notable exceptions include Bietak
and Engelmayer 1963; Bietak 1966, 1968), and the recent resurgence
of urban archeology (Kemp 1972a; Kemp and O'Connor 1974; O'Connor
1974; Bietak 1975) has had insufficient opportunity to stimulate
a fresh interest in the origins of Egyptian civilization.

It therefore comes as no surprise that the cross-cultural
debates of the ecological, demographic, and social processes basic
to emergent civilizations have increasingly ignored critical
Egyptian evidence (see, for example, Kraeling and Adams 1960;
R. Adams 1966, 1974; Smith and Young 1972). At an earlier time,
Egyptian materials were central to Childe's desiccation hypothesis
for cultural innovation (1929, p. 42; Toynbee 1935, pp. 304 f.);

Wittfogel's hydraulic theory of Oriental despotism (1938, 1957);
Steward's search for environmental and cultural regularities in
the rise of civilizations (1955, pp. 178 ff.); Frankfort's
analysis of the role of religion in early Near Eastern political
development (1948, 1951); and White's theory of the state church
(1948, 1959, pp. 326 ff., pp. 360 ff.). These views have been
examined by Trigger (forthcoming) in his cogent analysis of the
ambivalent relationship between anthropology and Egyptology.
Trigger explains the reluctance of Egyptologists to borrow from
or contribute to the social sciences by an introspective emphasis
on content rather than context. Whatever the reasons, the almost
traditional isolation of Egyptology has not served either archeology or anthropology well.

Despite their shortcomings, the totality of ancient Egyptian
records is unique for a time range that constitutes "prehistory"
almost everywhere else. This unusual wealth of data, which has
sustained an autonomous and vigorous field for so long, is primarily
the product of a diverse and comparatively well-preserved archeological record, and of an imperfect yet extensive corpus of written
records. Potentially, therefore, the Egyptian evidence should
allow unusual insights into the emergence of one of the earliest
high civilizations. Equally pertinent is that the complementary
nature of archeological and written data documents in unparalleled
fashion a five-thousand-year span of settlement, and in remarkable
detail. Nonetheless, these sources, well analyzed in terms of
their content, and certainly adequate for a unique perspective
on settlement continuity and change, remain to be exploited in
a broader context.

The purpose of this study is to examine the emergence of a
floodplain civilization in the Egyptian Nile Valley, viewed as
a test case of man-land relationships. The emergence of the first
high civilizations at the threshold of history has long been a
focus of great interest, but it has proved to be an elusive theme.
Much like the parallel problem of urban origins, with which it is
sometimes (incorrectly) equated, the slender informational base
has been manipulated in many ways to conform with a variety of
sociological and political paradigms. Intensive floodplain
subsistence is first and foremost an ecological phenomenon, yet
any ecological assessments have been casual, primitive, and often
deterministic. In my view, the Egyptian evidence has unusual
potential for a more discriminating evaluation of the fundamental

ecological interrelationships. The geographical framework can
be delineated with some confidence, and the temporal variability
of environmental parameters is amenable to systematic study.
The gradual development of irrigation agriculture can be inferred
from various lines of investigation. Settlement patterns within
the floodplain can be resolved to the extent that demographic
gradients and temporal trends are discernible.

I have tried to develop these themes as constructively as
the data allow, realizing that I have often ventured where more
qualified Egyptologists have feared to tread. But understanding
rather than perfection is the goal of scholarship, and we must
continue to reformulate and assess problems with the data in hand.
The results must speak for themselves. In this case, they are no
more conclusive than in any other study of historical processes.
They do, however, attest to the value of an ecological perspective
on a complex corpus of information, and the potential implications
for Egypt and other hydraulic civilizations are often surprising
and sometimes provocative.

AGRIGULTURAL ORIGINS IN THE NILE VALLEY

It is widely held that those plant and animal domesticates
that dominated ancient Egyptian agriculture were derived from
Southwest Asia. In particular, radiocarbon dating has shown that
cultigens and livestock first appeared in Egypt several millennia
after they did elsewhere in the Near East, and that the spectrum
of domesticates was closely modeled on that of southwestern Asia
(Helbaek 1959; Zeuner 1963; Harlan and Zohary 1966; Reed 1969;
Dixon 1969; Zohary and Hopf 1973). The general argument is, then,
that early agriculture diffused to Egypt or was brought there by
invaders from Asia, to replace an existing hunting-and-gathering
economy.

The radiocarbon dates now available, as well as the archeological surveys of the 1960s, lend a measure of support to this
view. Epi-Paleolithic occupance in the Faiyum is linked to a
sedimentary unit that is dated from before 8100 to shortly
after 7140 radiocarbon years ago (B.P. or "before present").[1]
Corrected for radiocarbon flux, this places a *terminus post quem*
of 6000 B.C. for the appearance of agriculture in northern
Egypt. In Nubia, preceramic Epi-Paleolithic industries related
to hunter-gatherer economies were exclusive until at least six
thousand radiocarbon years ago, that is, about 5000 B.C., subsequently overlapping with Neolithic sites for at least a

1. The "Premoeris" Lake is dated by I-4128 (8100 ± 130
B.P.), I-4126 (8070 ± 130 B.P.), I-4130 (7500 ± 125 B.P.), and
I-4129 (7140 ± 120 B.P.) (Said, Albritton, et al. 1972).

TABLE 1 Chronological Framework for Ancient Egypt

Hellenistic (332 B.C. - A.D. 641)
Roman-Byzantine Period (30 B.C. - A.D. 641)
Ptolemaic Period (323 - 30 B.C.)

Dynastic (2700 - 332 B.C.)
Late Period (including Libyan, Ethiopian, and Saite dynasties)
(1070 - 332 B.C.)
New Kingdom (including Amarna and the Ramessid Era) (1570 -
1070 B.C.)
Second Intermediate Period (including Hyksos Era) (1715 -
1570 B.C.)
Middle Kingdom (including 12th Dynasty) (2040 - 1715 B.C.)
First Intermediate Period (including 7th to 10th dynasties)
(2250 - 2040 B.C.)
Old Kingdom (Pyramid Age) (2700 - 2215 B.C.)

Early Dynastic (3050 - 2700 B.C.)

Predynastic (5200 - 3050 B.C.)
Late Predynastic Assemblages (including Nagada culture [Amratian
and Gerzean, 4600 - 3050 B.C.] , isolated northern sites,
and Nubian A-Group [3600 - 2900 B.C.])
Early Predynastic Assemblages (including Merimde [4900 - 4500
B.C.] , Faiyum "A" [4700 - 4000 B.C.] , Badarian [5200 -
4600 B.C.] , and Nubian Ceramic Neolithic [5000 - 3600 B.C.])

Epi-Paleolithic industries, until after 6000 B.C. in northern
Egypt and as late as 4000 B.C. in parts of Nubia

SOURCE: Calibrated radiocarbon and thermoluminescent assays prior
to ca. 2700 B.C., and based on unpublished notes of Klaus Baer,
Charles Van Siclen, and Edward Wente for the Dynastic era.

NOTE: The 7th and 8th dynasties have been included in the First
Intermediate Period as a matter of convenience, although this
and any dates prior to ca. 2000 B.C. are the subject of considerable differences of opinion among various authors.

millennium[2] (table 1).

The oldest radiocarbon dates for "Neolithic" sites were obtained on the Delta margins at Merimde, and from scattered lakeshore settlements in the Faiyum Depression. Corrected for radiocarbon flux, and all subsequent B.C. assays quoted here have been so calibrated after Ralph, Michael, and Han (1973), they seem to argue for an introduction of agriculture to northern Egypt a little before 5000 B.C. In particular, the corrected, 2σ range for seven concordant dates from Merimde is 4900-4500 B.C.,[3] for three recently obtained dates for the Faiyum "A," 4660-4000 B.C.[4] El-Omari, another Neolithic site near Cairo, may date ca. 3900 B.C. on the basis of the questionable solid carbon method.[5] The equally uncertain assays on various Gerzean or Nagada II (Late Chalcolithic) sites in the Nile Valley have a simple range from 4690-3010 B.C.,[6] with a firmer lower limit set by the maximum, acceptable radiocarbon age of 3060 ± 50 B.C. on the early 1st Dynasty.[7] In Lower Nubia, "pottery Neolithic" of unconfirmed relevance to early agriculture dates ca. 5000-3600 B.C.[8] Independent thermoluminescent dates on potsherds, also to be evaluated with due caution, are now available for both the Gerzean and Badarian (Early Chalcolithic) of Upper Egypt (Whittle 1975). The former (four assays) range from 4360-3775 B.C., the latter

2. The youngest date on the Qadan, a microlithic flake industry, is 6430 ± 200 B.P. (Wendorf 1968, pp. 1050 f.); on the Arkinian, a microlithic blade industry, 9390 ± 100 B.P. (Wendorf 1968, pp. 1051 f.); on the "Mesolithic" from Abka, similar to the Qadan, 9175 ± 400 B.P. (Derricourt 1971). The Shamarkian, a microlithic flake and bladelet industry, has dates of 7700 ± 120 B.P. and 5220 ± 50 B.P. (Wendorf 1968, pp. 1052 f.), the latter apparently overlapping in age with ceramic sites.

3. U-6 to U-10, U-31, U-73 (see Derricourt 1971).

4. I-4127, I-4131, and BM-530 (Said et al. 1972; Barker et al. 1971).

5. C-463 (see Derricourt 1971).

6. C-810 to C-814 (see Derricourt 1971).

7. For a compilation and discussion of more refined radiocarbon assays on the 1st Dynasty, see Derricourt (1971), particularly his figure 3.

8. Soleb necropolis, P-721 and P-722, 4905 and 4980 B.C.; Catfish Cave, Y-1680, 3520 B.C.; Afyeh, UW-30, 4410 B.C.; Dibeira West 50, WSU-174, 4370 B.C.; Abka, M-801 to M-803, 3140 - 4610 B.C.; Karagan, GX-423, 3625 B.C. (see Derricourt 1971; Wendorf 1968, p. 1053).

(six assays), 5580-4330 B.C.--all with a stated error range of
± 5%. Interpreted literally, these Badarian assays would infer
a minimum age spread of 5160-4685 B.C., and a greater age for
food production in southern rather than northern Egypt.

The implications are that Merimde and Faiyum "A," in northern
Egypt, and the Badarian further south, date mainly to the fifth
millennium B.C. The Gerzean and at least some of the early Nubian
ceramic sites pertain primarily to the fourth millennium. No
older "Neolithic" sites have been found in the Nile Valley, and
it is noteworthy that earlier cultural strata are indubitably
those of "Mesolithic" or "Epi-Paleolithic" artifact assemblages
that argue for hunting, fishing, and gathering economies (see
Schild, Chmielewska, and Wieckowska 1968; Shiner 1968; Butzer
and Hansen 1968, pp. 187 ff.; Vermeersch 1970; Said, Albritton,
et al. 1972; Wendorf and Schild 1975).

Why the apparent cultural lag of Egypt behind southwestern
Asia? McBurney (1960, pp. 142 ff.) essentially reformulated
older views (see Caton-Thompson 1946), implying that Stone Age
Egypt was culturally "unprogressive." This was, however, possible
only by downplaying the antiquity of Vignard's Sebilian sequence
near Kom Ombo, where grinding stones were found in very early
contexts (Vignard 1923; Huzayyin 1941; Smith 1968; Butzer and
Hansen 1968, pp. 143 ff., 180 ff.). Wendorf and Said (1967)
subsequently resuscitated the grinding stones, as possible
evidence for agriculture as early as 14,000 B.P. A more seasoned
reassessment has now been offered by Wendorf and Schild (1975),
who show that numerous grinding stones and lustrous-edged blades
(probably sickles) begin to appear in the record ca. 14,500 B.P.,
and that a sequence near Isna, dated ca. 12,700-12,000 B.P., has
large Gramineae pollen that imply cereals and may well represent
(wild?) barley. Interestingly, these "proto-agricultural" features
are far less prominent in sites younger than 11,500 B.P.

Whatever the ultimate merits of the Wendorf-Schild argument,
it shows clearly that Egypt was not unprogressive prior to 5000
B.C. and it calls for another look at the evidence. Hilzheimer
(1926, 1930) and Boessneck (1953, 1960) have already drawn attention to the indigenous flavor of ancient Egyptian agriculture,
including the local strains that dominated in cattle, pig, donkey,
dog, and cat breeding; the keeping or semidomestication of the
ichneumon, gazelle, oryx, addax, ibex, and hyena; as well as the
individuality of the poultry, particularly the geese and ducks.

Clark (1971) has accordingly formulated a partially speculative
sequence for Egypt:

    1. Intensive hunting and collecting, ca. 17,000-11,000 B.P.,
with increased emphasis on fish, birds, and wild grains and seeds;

    2. Possible indigenous domestication of some large, local
mammals (for example, cattle)[9] and of seed grasses, such as
Aristida, *Eragrostis*, *Panicum*, and particularly *Echinochloa*,
prior to 5000 B.C.;

    3. Introduction of more successful winter-rainfall crops
(emmer and barley) and herd animals (sheep, goat, pig, possibly
cattle) from Asia to Egypt, where they were rapidly incorporated
by an already receptive economy to become the regular agricultural
staples;

    4. Experimentation with the local mammals and avifauna as
well as use of minor, local grains (*Echinochloa*) persisting
through the Old Kingdom, long after the switch from "dry farming" (*sic* Clark 1971, fig. 2) to intensive irrigation agriculture.

    Altogether there now are substantial grounds to reconsider
the individuality of ancient Egyptian agriculture, both with respect to its Asiatic affinities, and in regard to the broader
cultural sphere of Saharan Africa. The fact is that the available
"hard" evidence for agriculture in the Nile Valley is not only
later than that in Asia, but also two millennia later than that
from the moister Saharan hill country (Mori 1965; Camps 1969;
Maitre 1971).[10] A similar gradient can be observed in the Maghreb,
where the Capsian populations of the moister Atlas country adopted
certain Neolithic traits 1,000 years later than the advent of
agriculture on the adjacent Mediterranean lowlands, and as much as
2,000 years later than the Saharan Capsian foci (Camps 1975;
Camps, Délibrias, and Thommeret 1973; Butzer 1971a, pp. 585 ff.).

    9.   Hassan (1972) also suspects that cattle herding was well
established in Egypt prior to the introduction of Asiatic forms.
On one hand, domesticated cattle are conspicuously absent in the
"Fertile Crescent" at sites such as Tepe Sabz, Banahilk, Amuq,
Tell Mureybit, Beisamun, and Hagoshrim prior to the fifth
millennium. On the other hand, cattle cults figure prominently
in the Saharan rock art, as well as in Predynastic and Dynastic
Egypt. Comparable cattle cults of greater antiquity are only known
from Anatolia.

    10.   This apposition was very recently confirmed in the
Libyan Desert, where domesticated cattle and sheep or goat have
been found with celts and Early Khartum pottery at Nabta Playa,
south of Kharga Oasis; the ten C^{14} dates lie within one standard
deviation of 6000 B.C. (uncalibrated) (Fred Wendorf, personal communication).

To explain this pattern it must be noted that both the Atlas
Capsians and the pre-Neolithic occupants of the Nile Valley
practiced a conspicuously intensive, broad-spectrum hunting-and-
gathering economy. I feel that in these ecologically favored
habitats such food-collecting economies were so successful and
efficient that local groups cognizant of agricultural or pastoral
traits among some of their neighbors initially refused to change
their own way of life (Butzer 1971a, p. 591).[11] As Boserup
(1965, p. 41) has argued, people may well be aware of the existence of more intensive methods of land use, yet prefer to ignore
such technology until population size is such that a lower output
per man-hour must be accepted.

In effect, the Nile Valley proved resistant to early Neolithic intrusions from both the Mediterranean borderlands and
the Saharan hill country and oases, despite the inherent suit-
ability of the floodplain and delta to farming (see below).
When Neolithic traits were finally adopted, at a relatively late
date, efficient primary village-agriculture had already been
fully established in southwestern Asia for some time. Whatever
its intellectual and material antecedents, an economy based
largely on food production finally appeared in northern Egypt
shortly before 5000 B.C. Several explanations are possible, including autochthonous development of agriculture in the Nile
Valley, adoption and adaptation of agricultural traits by nilotic
populations, or an actual influx of settlers from without. In
terms of diffusion or migration, external impulses could potentially have been derived from southwestern Asia via Sinai or the
Red Sea, from the western deserts and steppes, or from the Sudan.
Several lines of argumentation can be utilized, including the
domesticates themselves, biological changes of the human populations, the archeological assemblages, and the linguistic heritage.

---

11. A possible additional factor has been noted by Hassan
(1972). A series of exceptionally high floods swept the Nile
Valley ca. 11,500-11,000 B.P. (Butzer and Hansen 1968, pp. 115,
129, 278; Butzer, Issac, et al. 1972), after which Hassan notes
a reduction in the number of settlements, population size, and
artifact stylistic traditions. These catastrophic events may
have discouraged the trend toward an agricultural economy, favoring instead an emphasis on gathered riverine resources.

The standard domesticates characteristic of Egyptian agriculture in the Predynastic era and Old Kingdom belong to the as-
semblage almost generally attributed to southwestern Asia and,
possibly, the Aegean borderlands (see Bender 1975, with sources).
However, domesticated cattle, sheep, and emmer wheat were well
known along the North African coasts and in the Saharan highlands
at least a millennium earlier, and it is probable that goat, pig,
barley, and flax were also well established in other parts of
northern Africa long before 5000 B.C.

The physical anthropological evidence is inconclusive, in
part on account of the absence of Epi-Paleolithic skeletal remains
from Egypt proper, in part also because of the woefully inadequate
study of the once-abundant Predynastic cemetery record in Egypt.
The Epi-Paleolithic populations of Nubia were unusually robust
but the cemetery record of dental change through time, for example, could be explained without resort to migrations by a reduction in tooth size and complexity through selection for caries-
resistant teeth (Greene 1972). For the Predynastic period, broad
similarities between Egyptians (see Batrawi 1946-47; Berry,
Berry, and Ucko 1967) and their Nubian counterparts neither prove
nor disprove genetic relationships (Greene 1972).

The archeological record is more informative. In the south,
in Upper Nubia, dotted wavy-line pottery of Khartum type overlaps
in time with the latest Epi-Paleolithic, but the associated lithic
assemblages are clearly different and intrusive (Wendorf and
Schild 1975; also Wendorf 1968, pp. 1051 ff.). The earliest
known agricultural site within the modern boundaries of Egypt
is related to the Khartum Variant, and found in the southern
Libyan Desert (see footnote 10 above). Although one Epi-Paleolithic group, the Abkan of the Second Cataract, acquired pottery
manufacture while retaining a local lithic tradition, the Khartum
Neolithic appears to play no significant role in early agriculture within the Egyptian Nile Valley. In the north, the Faiyum
"A," linked to Merimde by its bifacial knives and concave-based
arrowheads (J. L. Phillips, personal communication), is macro-
lithic and quite distinct from all preceding and coeval microlithic traditions in the Nile Valley, both on technological and
typological grounds (see Said, Albritton, et al. 1972; Wendorf
and Schild 1975). This argues for an intrusive origin of the
Neolithic and, ultimately, Predynastic, involving migration
rather than trait diffusion or local innovation. Significantly,

however, this new lithic tradition finds no parallels in Sinai
or the Levant (J. L. Phillips, personal communication), precluding
immigration from that sector. If anything, the only plausible
technological roots of the strong Neolithic-Predynastic bifacial
tradition would be in the North African Aterian of the late
Pleistocene. This does not, of course, preclude the probability
of later Asiatic influences, such as the introduction of metal-
lurgy.

The linguistic evidence also does not support a hybrid between
a Semitic overlay and an African substratum, but instead argues
for ancient Egyptian as a distinct branch of the Afro-Asiatic language family (Greenberg 1955, pp. 43 ff.).[12]

The sum total of the evidence consequently favors an introduction of the Neolithic, but from a northwestern rather than
northeastern source. The new groups involved were intrusive,
but they were North African, and they may have come from the
oases of the northern Libyan Desert or further west in the Sahara,
or along the Mediterranean littoral. Both the Faiyum "A" and
the Khartum Variant economies included strong hunting, fishing,
and gathering components. This points to a subsistence pattern
already preadapted ecologically to riverine, lacustrine or spring
oases, much like the previous Nile Valley cultures had been. Many
of the domesticates probably were not new, but the partial
emphasis on food production was. The persistence of strong hunting, gathering, and fishing components, as well as the only
gradual displacement of Epi-Paleolithic technology in Upper Egypt
and Nubia, argues that the new economic modes were adopted slow-
ly and selectively during a millennium or more, rather than
dramatically. The agricultural system in effect in late Predynastic times, prior to 3050 B.C., consequently had a long and
complex evolution. It was presumably well adapted to the peculiar-
ities of the nilotic environment, with its summer floods, and
autumn to winter growing season. Its roots must be sought in
both Africa and Asia, from among a wide array of economic and
cultural traditions.

12. Although glottochronology is rightly suspect, the divergence of Old Kingdom Egyptian and Akkadian in the third
millennium B.C. could be used to argue for an original separation
of the Afro-Asiatic languages perhaps 2,000 years earlier (see
Trigger 1968, p. 74), with Egypt itself as a possible candidate
for the place of origin for this language family. In any event,
there is as yet no reason to doubt that the Predynastic peoples
of the Egyptian Nile Valley already spoke Egyptian.

3

ECOLOGY AND PREDYNASTIC SETTLEMENT OF THE FLOODPLAIN AND DELTA

Misconceptions have persistently marred discussion of early
"colonization" of the Nile floodplain and delta. As explicitly
formulated by Willcocks (1904, pp. 65 f.), Newberry (1925), and
Childe (1929, pp. 42, 46), and restated in a broader context by
Toynbee (1935, pp. 304 f.), the basic argument is as follows:
1. Pre-agricultural settlement was originally limited to
what is now desert because of a "pluvial" climate that accompanied
the Pleistocene glacials; the Nile bottomlands at this time were
postulated to be an inaccessible morass of swampland and jungle,
whereas the delta had barely begun to build up into the sea.
2. As the Pleistocene glaciers waned and rains became infre-
quent, people and animals were attracted to the water and permanent
sustenance offered by the Nile floodplain; this trend was favored
by a partial emergence of the Nile marshes as the rains over
Ethiopia declined, bringing gentler inundations.
3. Predynastic settlers, from a base on the floodplain margins, during the fifth and fourth millennia B.C. tackled the
hydraulic problems of the bottomlands by draining the swamps,
cutting down the thickets, and inaugurating irrigation projects;
a similar process of land "reclamation" was begun in the deltaic
wastes a little later, in Old Kingdom times (ca. 2700-2215 B.C.),
and only completed under the Ptolemies (323-30 B.C.).

These notions reflect the paleoclimatic understanding of
the 1920s, insufficient data on the nature of pre-Neolithic settlement in Egypt, confusion between a free-draining floodplain and
the Sudd swamps of the central Sudan, misconceptions regarding
floodplain irrigation, and inadequate geomorphologic information
from the Nile Delta. Present information on these points will
be discussed in turn.

Prehistoric Climates of Egypt

Rainfall in the Libyan Desert and the Red Sea Hills has
been insufficient to sustain any appreciable population, except
in the vicinity of springs or wadis with high watertables, since
at least 30,000 to 50,000 years ago (Butzer 1975a). About 25,000-
17,000 B.P. the climate of Egypt was as dry as today, while the
floodplain was also comparable but almost twice as wide and prone
to more violent flood surges (Butzer and Hansen 1968, pp. 97 ff.,
149, 272 ff.). Then, ca. 17,000-8000 B.P., there were more frequent winter rains in Egypt, primarily restricted to the Red Sea
Hills, but providing discharge and, accordingly, fringing vegetation and groundwater resources to wadis draining to the Nile
margins (Butzer and Hansen 1968, pp. 149, 280 ff., 328; Butzer
1959b). The Nile itself was characterized by more vigorous summer
floods, with the competence to carry massive loads of coarse gravel
from Nubia to Cairo, and derived from rains over Ethiopia or the
central Sudan (Butzer and Hansen 1968, pp. 107 ff., 149, 274 ff.,
328, 330 ff., 456; 1972).

Relatively frequent, gentle rains allowed the development
of a reddish soil in the Egyptian deserts ca. 5000 B.C. (Butzer
and Hansen 1968, pp. 121, 304 ff., 328, 333, 488 ff.), while during
the fourth millennium occasional heavy rains promoted strong surface runoff that eroded this soil or buried it under extensive
sheets of stony rubble (Butzer and Hansen 1968, pp. 121 ff.,
288 f., 304 ff., 331 ff.). Meanwhile, the trend of Nile floods
from 6000-3000 B.C. can best be deduced from the record of the
Faiyum, with its alternating high lakes (strong flood influx via
the Hawara channel) and temporary recessions (limited influx across
that threshold). These floods were relatively low ca. 6000-
5000 B.C., high ca. 5000-3700 B.C., then temporarily lower, with
another major episode of high floods and accelerated alluviation
culminating about 3000 B.C. (see Said, Albritton, et al. 1972;
Butzer and Hansen 1968, pp. 276 ff.; Säve-Söderbergh 1964). The
moister climate prevailing in late Predynastic and Early Dynastic
time supported a considerable and diversified fauna in and along
the margins of the Nile Valley, as well as in the Red Sea Hills
(Butzer 1958, 1959b, pp. 78 ff.).

Localization of Prehistoric Settlement

In effect, the late prehistoric environmental history of
Egypt was complex and variable. Significant for human settlement

was that during most of the time between 15,000 and 3000 B.C.
the desert supported sufficient game to allow hunting groups at
least a seasonal livelihood, while the "desert-savanna" vegetation, which must be assumed for all but the core of the Libyan
Desert, was suitable for modest seasonal exploitation by herds-
men from the Nile Valley or nomadic pastoralism by small, desert-
based groups.

Coeval archeological vestiges are logically concentrated
within the former Nile floodplain (Wendorf 1968, pp. 1044 ff.;
Butzer and Hansen 1968, pp. 163 ff., 181 ff.; Phillips and
Butzer 1975; Hassan 1975; Wendorf and Schild 1975; Trigger 1965,
pp. 66 ff.), near adjacent "quartzite" or flint quarry localities
such as the Theban hillsides (see also Caton-Thompson 1952, pp.
187 ff., and for good Middle Paleolithic examples, Guichard and
Guichard 1965), in spring-fed oases (Caton-Thompson 1952, pp.
145 ff.; Butzer and Hansen 1968, pp. 389 ff.; Hobler and Hester
1969), around the shores of lakes (Caton-Thompson and Gardner
1929) or ephemeral, rain-fed ponds (Caton-Thompson 1952, pp. 158
ff.; Hobler and Hester 1969; Schild and Wendorf 1975), and along
the wadis of the desert hill country (Winkler 1938-39; Butzer
and Hansen 1968, pp. 183 ff.; McHugh 1975).

The apparent restriction of Badarian and Nagadan settlement sites to the desert margins of the floodplain[1] may relate
to seasonal pastoral activity by some segments of the population
outward into the desert (see, for example, O'Connor 1972b;
Fairservis 1972; Hoffman 1972). However, there is no discernible,
systematic contrast in the foci of Paleolithic versus Neolithic
settlement, despite the change of subsistence patterns. Admit-
tedly the Nile built up and expanded its floodplain at times of
stronger floods, and then reverted to cutting out a lower-lying
and narrower alluvial plain during intervals of weak floods.
Yet the great bulk of all Paleolithic materials recovered from
Egypt come from deposits of the Nile River, and--whatever their

1. The question may be raised whether there were any Predynastic groups that did not utilize desert cemeteries. The frequency of desert-edge cemeteries in Nubia, where the floodplain
is very narrow and discontinuous, suggests that floodplain cemeteries were rare or absent. However, the broad Egyptian floodplain is another matter, and here the desert margin cemeteries
and settlement sites (Kaiser 1961; Butzer 1960b, 1961) are far
too few to be considered the rule rather than the exception
(Butzer 1959c).

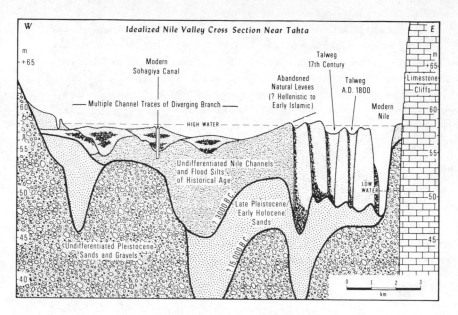

Fig. 1.--Idealized Nile Valley cross section near Tahta, province of Sohag.

present location and elevation--they derive from settlements originally situated next to that river.

Geomorphology and Hydrology of the Nile Floodplain
    The Nile Valley is a seasonally inundated river plain, not a swamp basin as most recently argued by Baumgartel (1947, pp. 3, 49, 55; commentaries in Arkell and Ucko 1965, pp. 156 f.) and Arkell and Ucko (1965, p. 162). For this reason the valley bottomlands have been a center of settlement from time immemorial. During the last 25,000 years the alluvial deposits laid down by the Nile in Nubia and Egypt consist of sandy or gravelly channel beds that interfinger laterally with silts and clays due to flood-waters that spill over the banks seasonally (Butzer and Hansen 1968, pp. 107 ff., 274 ff.).
    In terms of floodplain types, that of the Nile has always been of the "convex" variety (see, for example, Leopold, Wolman, and Miller 1964, pp. 316 ff.), accumulating primarily through bank overflow of suspended sediment (silt or clay), rather than

the "flat" variety, built up mainly in response to repeated
channel shifts and lateral accretion of bed load sediment (sand
or gravel) within such channels. A convex floodplain is marked
by natural levees that constitute the low-water channel banks
and that rise a few meters above the seasonally inundated alluvial
flats. The resulting valley cross section is slightly convex,
with the lowest areas distant from the river and often situated
near the outer margins of the valley. The Nile floodplain forms
a classic example of this type, as long recognized by irrigation
engineers but first explicated by Passarge (1940).

Examination of the detailed topographic maps of the Survey
of Egypt (for example, at scales of 1:100,000 or 1:25,000) shows
that the natural levees accompanying the Nile channel rise 1-3 m
above the lowest alluvial basins (see fig. 1). They have been
further raised and reinforced by artificial embankments that
serve as longitudinal dikes to contain the river. The alluvial
flats are not featureless but are often crisscrossed by low,
sinuous rises, commonly formed of abandoned levees that trace older
Nile channels. Additionally, these flats are transected by multiple canals as well as transverse dikes that are 3-4 m in height
and have a crown width of 6 m or so.

On broader floodplain segments, north of Nag Hammadi, a
secondary Nile channel or branch runs near the western margins
of the floodplain. The best known of these is the Bahr Yusef,
which now diverges from the Nile near Dairut, and formerly
branched off between Asyut and Manfalut to flow into the Faiyum.
The Bahr Yusef is repeatedly documented throughout the Islamic
era (see Toussoun 1925, pp. 174 ff., 253 ff.) and, despite repeated artificial modifications, both of its intake and its depth
(see Brown 1887), it is a natural meandering stream. It has a
sinuosity index (ratio of talweg length to that of meander-belt
axis) ranging from 1.25 to 1.90, which is considerably greater
than that of the Nile itself. Whereas the Nile channel averages
800-1,000 m in width and 10-12 m in depth, the Bahr Yusef is
typically 100 m wide and 4 m deep. The Sohagiya Canal, which
diverges at Sohag, and the now-defunct Bahguriya Canal, diverging near Nag Hammadi, had similar properties ca. 1800 A.D. (see
Jacotin 1826, sheets 10-12). These three major bifurcations
occur just below valley constrictions imposed by bedrock constraints to the valley; in each case the valley axis bends to
the right, with a divergent branch swinging leftward across the

widening floodplain immediately downstream. Except for return irrigation flow, these branches originally were seasonal streams that dried out in midwinter. Multiple abandoned channel traces and meander scars (Butzer 1959a, p. 48), the allusions of the classical authors (Diodorus 1:52; Strabo 17:1.4), as well as the sites of Ptolemaic and older settlements in their immediate prox- imity (for example, Aphroditopolis, Tanis, Oxyrhynchus, Heracle- opolis), verify that similar branches existed throughout the historical era.

The levees, both active and abandoned, of the Nile and its local branching channel served to divide the alluvial flats into discrete, natural flood basins. These were considerably larger than the artificially subdivided basins of the nineteenth and twentieth centuries, which averaged out by province and riverbank ranged from 9 sq km to 106 sq km (see Willcocks 1889, table 16, pp. 57 ff.), giving the typical west-bank basin an area of just under 35 sq km. Based on the valley sector between Girga and Asyut, it can be estimated that the natural flood basins would be two or three times as large, given the contemporary floodplain topography.

Under natural conditions the Nile would ideally rise to bankfull stage in southern Egypt by mid-August, and then spread out through major and minor overflow channels or by breaches across low levees, to spill over into successive flood basins. As the flood surge moved northward, the last basins at the north- ernmost end of the valley would be flooded four to six weeks later (see Willcocks and Craig 1913, p. 306). At the height of a normal flood, all but the crests of the levees would be briefly flooded, with average water depth in the flood basins about 1.5 m (Willcocks and Craig 1913, p. 305).[2] It is significant that with an average floodplain relief of only 2 m, exceptional one-in-ten- year floods would spill over the higher levees (Willcocks and Craig 1913, p. 304). During a poor flood some flood basins would remain dry, or otherwise the flood stage would be too brief or too low to allow flooding of the entire basin. After a span of

2. The common range of variability is 1-3 m, so that it is impossible to evaluate the (Old Kingdom ?) record of an average (?) or ideal (?) flood head of some 2.3 m (4 cubits, 3 palms, 3 1/3 digits) on the fields between Aswan and Memphis (see Lacau and Chevrier 1956, pl. 42; Gardiner 1944, p. 34).

several weeks or months, depending mainly on the relative elevation of the flood basins, the alluvial flats would emerge--
in response to a combination of falling riverhead, dropping groundwater level, evaporation, soil infiltration, and natural drainage back to the channel through small "gathering" streams. The
first basins in southern Egypt are normally dry by early October,
and by late November all but the lowest basin hollows in the
northernmost valley are drained, with persistent marsh in isolated, valley-margin backswamps or in the cutoff, oxbow lakes
of abandoned meanders.

The Sudd analogue is spurious since the Sudd is not a
floodplain but a former lake reduced to a vast marsh. The White
Nile--Bahr el-Ghazal lowlands have demarcated a great sedimentary basin since the late Tertiary (Whiteman 1971, pp. 88 ff.,
109 ff.). The surface of the Sudd is organic, rather than ter-
rigenous, as a floodplain would be. The low, swampy banks are
primarily built up of plant materials and rise only a half meter
or so above the dry-season water level of the lagoons that ac-
company the poorly defined stream channels (Hurst and Phillips
1931, pp. 75 ff., pl. 69 f.). Furthermore, the level of the
Sudd does not respond to a major "flood" season but remains relatively constant in relation to the double, equinoctial rainy
seasons of its catchment and the moderating influence of the East
African lakes. In other words, the physical geography of the
White Nile basin in general, and of the Sudd swamps in particular,
has little in common with the primeval Nile floodplain.

Natural vs. Artificial Floodplain Irrigation

The processes and features here described for the Nile
Valley are common to the floodplains of several major African
rivers. In particular, I have had opportunity to study them in
detail in the Omo Valley, a major Ethiopian river that responds
to rains and carries sediments comparable to those of the Nile,
but which is still relatively undisturbed by irrigation or large-
scale devegetation (Butzer 1971b). The seasonal inundation is
the dominant factor in plant growth in the Omo lowlands and
delta, so that vegetation analogies are also applicable, despite
the occurrence of sporadic but significant summer rains in this
semiarid rather than hyperarid environment. In particular,
there is a fringing, evergreen forest, including *Ficus*, *Zizyphus*
and trees of the acacia family, following the channels and

distributaries; the seasonally inundated flats are characterized
by grassland or *Acacia*-shrub savanna; wetland vegetation of
papyrus, reeds, or sedge is limited to the outer delta, along the
shores of Lake Rudolf (Carr, forthcoming; Butzer 1971b, pp. 16 ff.).

The contemporary land use of the Omo floodplain (Butzer
1971b, pp. 132 ff.), or that of the Senegal (Trochain 1940, pp.
173 ff.) and lower Chari-Logone (Erhart, Pias, and Leneuf 1954,
pp. 169 ff.) during the early twentieth century, is equally
relevant for the prehistoric Nile Valley. Crops are sown as the
late summer to early autumn flood waters recede, primarily between November and January. Despite an absence of "artificial"
irrigation, hygroscopic and capillary soil moisture, as well as
a high water table, permit crops to grow and mature during the
completely rainless winter months. Cultivation is practiced on
both the levees and the alluvial flats, whereas the dense, waterlogged soils of the backswamps are avoided. Settlements are restricted to or concentrated on the levees.

All the physical evidence indicates that the natural state
of the Nile Valley in prehistoric times closely resembled the
lower Omo, Senegal, Chari-Logone floodplains. The archeological
evidence from Nubia, and as regionally mapped for the Kom Ombo
Plain (Butzer and Hansen 1968, p. 184), shows that the great bulk
of the settlements must already have been concentrated on the
levees and immediate riverbanks during late Paleolithic times,
much as the subsequent Faiyum "A" groups clustered around the
lakeshores of the Faiyum (Caton-Thompson and Gardner 1934; Said,
Albritton, et al. 1972). There was no settlement shift from the
margins of the desert hills, the *khaset* land, into the fertile
floodplain, or *ta* land, after agriculture was introduced. Instead,
early farming communities continued to use the forested riverbanks for settlement sites, grazing animals in the grass and bush
country of the alluvial flats for eight or nine months of the
year, and planting their crops on the wet basin soils as the
floods receded. Big game was still frequent in the Nile, in the
thickets, and in the "land of the gazelles"--the open country
or desert, while fowl was abundant along the Nile or in the
"papyrus land"--amid the papyrus, reeds, and lotus pads of the
cutoff meanders, backswamps, or deltaic lagoons (see Butzer 1959b,
pp. 78 ff., 85 ff.; Woenig 1886; Lucas and Harris 1962, pp. 439 ff.;
Täckholm and Drar 1950, pp. 204 ff., 1954, pp. 529 ff.; Baumann
1960).

This was the early agricultural landscape of Egypt, with
natural irrigation, the "eotechnic" phase of Hamdan (1961). There
was no need for drainage to make the valley habitable. Furthermore, as long as the annual floods were persistently good, the
density of Predynastic population was probably insufficient to
warrant artificial irrigation. Given the natural flooding and
draining of the Nile floodplain, the average flood would allow
a single crop season over perhaps two-thirds of the alluvial surface.

The advantages of *artificial* irrigation were to increase
the area of the annual cropland in relation to variable flood
level, to retain water in the basins after undesirably brief flood
crests, to allow planting of new ground along the perimeter of
the floodplain, and to permit a second or even a third crop in
intensively utilized garden plots. These are then refinements
on a natural system of irrigation, the efficiency of which can be
greatly improved by a relatively limited input of labor. This first
level of improvement would include the annual dredging or deepening of the natural, diverging overflow channels; the digging of
short ditches to breach the low points of natural levees; blocking off the gathering streams by earthen dams; and the use of
buckets to raise water manually from residual ponds or natural
channels to adjacent fields.

Although agriculture was practiced for almost two millennia
before the political unification of Upper and Lower Egypt (ca.
3050 ± 50 B.C.), the earliest evidence for artificial irrigation
is the mace-head of the Scorpion King that shows one of the last
Predynastic kings ceremonially cutting an irrigation ditch
(Emery 1961, pp. 42 f., 236; Edwards 1971). Whether this representation symbolizes the simple cutting of a levee, as is
suggested by analogy to later ceremonies (see Lane 1860, pp. 501
ff.), or the excavation of a more elaborate canal system is immaterial. The lower panels of the mace-head, isasfar as preserved (fig. 2), indisputably show a waterway (represented in
traditional wavy-line pattern for water) that bifurcates toward
two grid networks, one of which is surmounted by a stylized but
unmistakable palm tree. The upper network, in analogy with 18th-
Dynasty garden representations, refers to four rows of rectangu-
lar, irrigated fields. The king is shown holding a large hoe,
with attendants ready with traditional fiber basket and broom.
Two other workmen, hoes in hand, appear to be excavating or

Fig. 2.--The Scorpion King inaugurating an irrigation network, ca. 3100 B.C. Drawn from photographs in Quibell (1900, pl. 26c) and Asselberghs (1961, pl. 172-76).

deepening the lower canal.[3] This significant document leaves little doubt that the transition from natural to modified and, ultimately, artificially regulated irrigation had been completed by the end of the Predynastic era.

3. It is difficult to accept Baumgartel's (1966) argument that this scene represents the king laying the foundations for a temple (!).

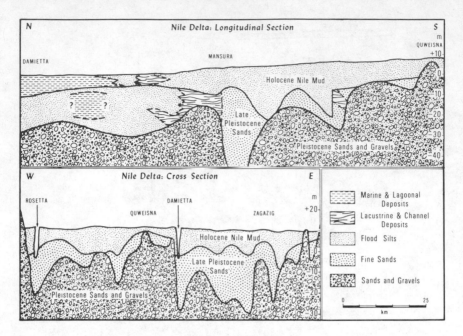

Fig. 3.--The Delta subsurface as seen in longitudinal and transverse sections. Modified after Butzer (1974, fig. 1).

Geomorphology of the Delta

The situation of the Nile Delta is both similar and anomalous
to that of the Nile Valley (Butzer 1974). The coastal perimeter
is today formed by cuspate subdeltas (Rosetta and Damietta),
beach ridges, and bay bars, the last cutting off brackish lagoons
(Maryut, Idku, Burullus, Manzala) from the open Mediterranean.
Extensive salt marshes, in part due to occasional flooding by
the sea, lie south of these lagoons as far as the 2-m contour.
However, the greatest part of the delta plain is a system of Nile
distributary branches, natural levees, alluvial flats (subdivided
into flood basins), and gathering streams (now artificial drains).
Divergence of flood waters over multiple distributaries produces
lower flood crests than in the valley upstream of Cairo, so that
the delta levees are correspondingly lower, with many basins
prone to forming seasonal or perennial swamps under natural
conditions.

Nonetheless, the subsurface geology shows that older views,
favoring a very recent age for seaward progradation of the delta

(Ball 1939, pp. 37 f.; R.W. Fairbridge, comments in Arkell and
Ucko 1965, p. 159), are now untenable. A vertical column of some
3,000 m of nilotic sediments has accumulated in the area of the
present delta since the late Miocene, with continued downwarping
of the underlying crust with the accumulating weight (Emery and
Bentor 1960; Harrison 1955; Soliman and Faris 1964; Said and
Yousri 1968; I.S. Chumakov in Butzer and Hansen 1968, pp. 521 f.).
Periodic erosion accompanied intervals of low Pleistocene sea
level, when the Mediterranean Sea was almost 150 m lower than
today--as recently as 20,000 years ago (see Curray et al. 1970).
On the basis of interpretation of over 250 bore profiles (see
Attia 1954) the three uppermost sedimentary units of the delta
can be defined and their contact planes reconstructed (fig. 3).
The results and Sestini's (forthcoming; Misdorp and Sestini,
forthcoming) recent studies show that, between 7000 and 4000
B.C., when the Mediterranean Sea rose from -20 m to near the
present level, the northern third of the Delta was reduced to a
vast tract of swamp and lagoon (fig. 3 and 4).[4] Rapid alluviation by the Nile, at an average rate of some 20 cm per century,
evidently compensated for this marine incursion by building a
10- to 40-m thick sheet of mud out over a delta that shortly after
4000 B.C. had reached approximately its present dimensions.

Predynastic delta topography can be reconstructed with some
confidence by plotting the thickness of recent Nile mud from the
borings, supplemented by satellite photography (see, for example,
Pouquet 1969), and modern topographic maps (see, for example,
Bietak 1975). Extensive areas of surface sands or thin mud
accumulations (0-10 m) occur in the central and southern delta
(fig. 4), and sediment rates imply that these would have been
above flood level and, allowing for lateral water seepage and

4. Sestini's unpublished recent work includes ten boreholes
in the Lake Edku region, with radiocarbon dates, as well as
further bores from northeast of Lake Burullus, currently being
studied. The Edku profiles show 5-10 m of beach sands (probably
recording the last 2,000 years) over 10-15 m of clays, with
peaty layers. A basal peat dates ca. 5,000 radiocarbon years ago,
that is, nearly 4000 B.C. As in other major deltas, there is
no evidence for marine transgressions into what is the contemporary Delta. However, large areas now seaward of the modern 4-
or 5-m contour will have been marshland or lagoon during much or
most of the historical era. Publication of Sestini's full data
will greatly enhance our understanding of changing river and
coastal topography in the northernmost reaches of the Delta.

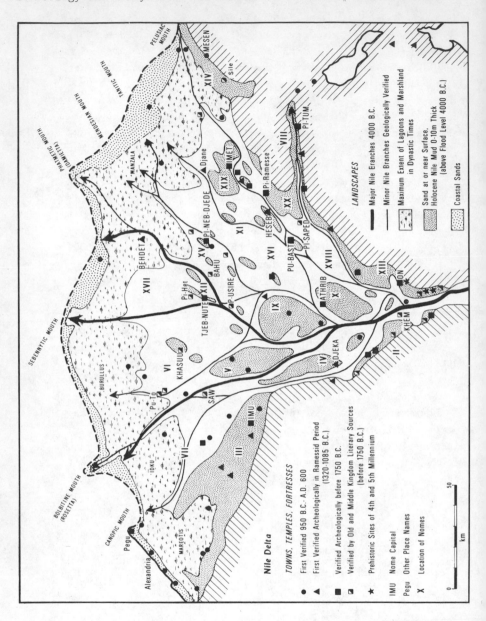

Fig. 4.--Landscape and settlement evolution in the Nile Delta. Based on Butzer (1974, fig. 2). The distributary network and relative importance of the major branches changed repeatedly during Dynastic and later times (for details, see Bietak 1975).

some winter rains, suitable only for grazing. These numerous
islands of dry land dotted a maze of distributaries and naturally draining flood basins, but with an increasing proportion of
marshland in the northern delta. Initially, three major Nile
branches are proven by subsurface topography, bifurcating near
Minuf and again at Samannud, leading to approximately the classic
Rosetta, Sebennytic, and Damietta mouths. In fact, Memphis, then
60 km (now 38 km) upstream of the delta apex, was on the banks
of the Nile. The seven or eight major distributaries verified
by Herodotus, Strabo, and Ptolemy ca. 450 B.C.-A.D. 150 (see
Ball 1942) only evolved during the third and second millennia B.C.
as the southern delta plain expanded, with some three--possibly
four or five--branches indicated during Ramessid times (1293-
1070 B.C.) (Bietak 1975).

Vegetation and land use of the delta plain in Predynastic
times were analogous to those of the Nile Valley. Apart from
the relatively late literary evidence, pollen spectra from a deep
coring below marshes 12 km south of Rosetta (Saad and Sami 1967)
show a logical abundance of reeds (*Phragmites*), bulrushes
(*Scirpus*), and papyrus (*Cyperus*), with hygrophytic ferns (*Riccia*),
cattail (*Typha*), and asphodel or lotus present, as well as tamarisk,
acacia, and a variety of dry-ground shrubs and weeds; yet from
the base of the recent Nile mud (here 11 m thick) upward, aquatics
declined as weeds and succulents (Euphorbiaceae) increased.

This picture of the Delta landscape contradicts the view of
Herodotus (II:4, 99), Baumgartel (1947, pp. 3 ff.), or J. A.
Wilson (in Kraeling and Adams 1960, p. 129) that the Predynastic
delta was an almost uninhabitable swampland. Endless lines of
levees and great expanses of sand islands or "turtlebacks"
(Butzer 1974; Kholief, Hilmy, and Shahat 1969) invited permanent
settlement, while seasonally flooded lands suitable for farming
or grazing were commonplace prior to large-scale drainage. Only
the northernmost delta was occupied by lagoons, swamps or salt
flats, much as it is today. Since 10 m of alluvium were deposited during the last 6,000 years, it is not surprising that there
is no Predynastic record from the delta proper.

4.

ENVIRONMENTAL PARAMETERS FOR THE DYNASTIC PERIOD

In view of what is now known about the late prehistoric era, it is to be expected that the environmental setting of Dynastic Egypt was also not immutable. Four categories of variability are of particular interest: (1) the changing climate of Egypt; (2) the short-term and long-term trends of the Nile floods; (3) the former topography of the Nile Valley; and (4) the role of environmental factors in modifying the landscapes of the Delta and the Faiyum. These aspects will be examined in turn and subsequently considered in terms of man-land interactions, in particular the role of technology and social organization in coping with the vagaries of the environment.

Final Desiccation of the Egyptian Deserts

Egypt enjoyed a slightly greater frequency and intensity of winter rains during Predynastic times, but during the first half of the third millennium B.C. the regional climate approached its present condition of hyperaridity. This must be deduced primarily from the absence of evidence to the contrary, although desiccation is apparent elsewhere in the Sahara at about the same time (Butzer 1971a, pp. 581 ff.; Butzer, Isaac, et al. 1972).

Of major significance in Egypt itself is the faunal and floral evidence provided by pictorial representations. Between the end of the 1st and the beginning of the 4th dynasties (ca. 2900-2600 B.C.), elephant, rhinoceros, giraffe, and gerenuk gazelle disappeared from the Nile Valley north of Aswan, and from the Red Sea Hills, to be increasingly restricted to the margins of the Nubian Nile (see, with reservation, Červiček 1973), to the summer rainfall belt along the southern fringes of the Sahara, or, in the case of the gerenuk, to the savannas of eastern

Africa (Butzer 1958, 1959b, pp. 96 ff.). At the same time the
camel became extinct throughout northern Africa (Murray 1952;
Mikesell 1955), while Barbary sheep, lion, and leopard became
decidedly scarce in Egypt. Uncertainty remains as to what
extent the relatively small local populations of elephant,
rhinoceros, and giraffe were simply destroyed by man. In fact,
their disappearance from the favorable environment of the floodplain itself can only be attributed to hunting and to competition
from herd animals. Their simultaneous, selective elimination
from the desert wadis, where large numbers of antelopes and other
more drought-adapted forms survived, nonetheless suggests that
an environmental factor was involved in both environments, but
in differing ways and to different degrees. It is interesting
that several 5th-Dynasty (ca. 2525-2400 B.C.) hunt scenes from
Saqqara and Abu Sir show scattered trees and shrubs on sandy
or rocky desert surfaces, implying a desert-savanna vegetation
within reasonable proximity of Memphis (Butzer 1959b, pp. 87f.).

A second faunal change is apparent, with addax, ibex, and
oryx becoming quite scarce during the 6th to 11th dynasties (ca.
2400-1991 B.C.). Thereafter the desert (as opposed to riverine)
game encountered in the art of the Middle and New kingdoms was
largely limited to the modest dorcas gazelle and the bubaline
hartebeest. Once again, eradication by man was certainly involved, but the survival of addax and oryx in the more mesic,
coastal desert steppe until the nineteenth century--despite
constant hunting predation --argues for an environmental input
as well.

The geological evidence shows that the balance of soil formation and erosion in the Egyptian deserts since the 1st Dynasty
was broadly comparable to that of today. This suggests that the
evidence of the representational art for faunal decimations
following the 1st Dynasty (after ca. 2850 B.C.) and during the
First Intermediate Period (ca. 2150 B.C.) were indeed, in part,
a response to deterioration of desert grazing.

Long- and Short-term Trends of Nile Floods

The evidence for variability of Nile flood level is even
more dramatic, despite the tantalizingly incomplete nature of
the records. These data have recently been analyzed in detail
by Bell (1970, 1971, 1975), and although her results do not claim
to be conclusive, they are nonetheless reasonably convincing.

For the Early Dynastic period and in the Old Kingdom there
are sixty-three annual flood records from eleven different rulers.
Although small in terms of sample size, when averaged per dynasty,
these flood levels show a general decline that was most rapid during
the late 1st and early 2nd Dynasty, that is ca. 3000-2800 B.C.
If one assumes a constant floodplain elevation, the difference is
in the order of 1 m; if the floodplain was simultaneously ag-
graded at a rate of 10 cm per century, this difference increases
to 1.6 m (Bell 1970). The lower of these two figures seems the
more probable, since declining floods would eventually lead to
floodplain incision, not progressive alluviation. A rough estimate of decreased Nile discharge can be made for a 1-m drop
of mean flood level by applying the approximate equivalents of
flood level and river volume applicable to Egypt (see Willcocks
1904, p. 150). Depending on exactly where the Nilometer was
located, the absolute levels involved, the degree to which the
decline affected all flood levels, and whether or not the inter-
mediate-level, preflood and postflood months were affected, the
decrease of mean discharge can be estimated at 29% ± 5%. Whatever the absolute figures, a substantial decline is involved,
and this written evidence consequently complements and explains
the record of Nile downcutting in Nubia, where the river incised
its floodplain by 6 m or more in late A-Group times (shortly
after 3000 B.C.) (see Butzer and Hansen 1968, pp. 276 ff.). The
new and lower floodplain eventually created in Egypt and Nubia
during the middle of the third millennium has persisted, with
relatively minor or localized natural modifications, until the
present day. In other words, the modern floodplain has existed
in its essentials since the Old Kingdom.

For the First Intermediate Period and early Middle Kingdom, Bell (1971; see also Vandier 1936) has reexamined a large
body of contemporaneous texts to deduce a series of catastrophical-
ly low floods between 2250 and perhaps 1950 B.C.[1] It is
debatable whether *all* of these references can be considered as

1.   The youngest of these famine years is recorded at Beni
Hasan and occurred during the lifetime of Ameni, who died in
1929 B.C.; this may possibly be the same famine referred to by
Mentuhotep, son of Hepi (see Schenkel 1962, pp. 114 f.).

historical rather than literary allusions to real, datable events.[2]
However, the sum total of the descriptions unquestionably serves
to document the range of physical and social repercussions of one
or more unusually severe ecological crises at the very end of
the Old Kingdom.

For the later Middle Kingdom, Bell (1975) argues from a care-
ful analysis of twenty-eight high flood records found in Nubia
that there must have been a good number of phenomenally high
floods during the short interval ca. 1840-1770 B.C. In the con-
fines of the Second Cataract, these floods were 9.0 m higher than
the average flood of the twentieth century, with a volume of
32×10^8 cu m per day--three times the mean peak volume of the
ten greatest floods of the late nineteenth century (Bell 1975).
Spread out over a much wider valley cross section at Aswan, such
a volume would produce a crest at least 4.5 m higher than the
modern mean, whereas the difference downstream would eventually
be reduced to perhaps 2 m. Although unusual, such aberrations
are possible, and find precedents in the catastrophic floods of
A.D. 1818-1819 (see Ball 1939, pp. 231 f.). A few score events
of this magnitude could not be expected to leave a geomorphic
record, but they would have had disrupting effects on agricultural
life.

No systematic study is yet available for the floods of the
New Kingdom and the Late Dynastic period (ca. 1570-332 B.C.).
In Egypt proper, there are, however, repeated (rather than isolated) records of exceptionally high floods from the ninth and
seventh centuries B.C. (see Ventre 1896; Beckerath 1966), and
floods may have been unusually good in the fifth century B.C.
as well as in the first century A.D. (Toussoun 1925, pp. 413 ff.).
However, for an earlier era it is relevant that, in the eastern
Delta, the declining discharge of the Pelusiac branch forced the
abandonment of the royal residence at Pi-Ramesse (Avaris) in
favor of Djane (Tanis) on the Tanitic branch shortly after 1200
B.C. (Bietak 1975, pp. 82 ff., 215 ff.). In Lower Nubia, de
Heinzelin's (1964) examination of the west-bank site of Aksha,
near Dibeira, serves to illustrate general trends. Here a temple of Ramses II was built on the floodplain at a time when average
floods were 1 m higher than today, with silts lapping up over

2. Klaus Baer: personal communication.

the foundations and adjacent dunes cultivated without the use of
lift irrigation (see de Heinzelin 1964, fig. 2). The area was
soon abandoned and later covered with eolian sands when Nile
floods were sufficiently low to permit salt efflorescences to form
in the temple precincts. These were already sufficiently thick
to merit commercial removal early in the Meroitic period (ca.
300 B.C.-A.D. 250). Nile flood levels increased after A.D. 600
(Adams 1965) to allow cultivation among the dunes at Aksha, from
A.D. 800-1000. A second eolian episode terminated only when introduction of the saqiya permitted recolonization of the dune
fields (de Heinzelin 1964). The Aksha evidence indicates a sustained decline of Nile flood levels after perhaps 1200 B.C. on a
scale sufficient to promote floodplain dissection, with net ag-
gradation not in evidence again until well into the Christian era.[3]

All in all, the available Egyptian records document both an
appreciable degree of short-term variability and significant long-
term trends of the Nile over a five-thousand-year period. Since
the Nile reflects climatic trends in the summer monsoonal rainfall
belt of Ethiopia and the central Sudan, as well as in the region
of equinoctial rains in East Africa (see Butzer 1971b, chap. 5),
an independent record of potential moisture trends is provided by
a number of regional studies during the last decade or so. A
general parallelism of high and low lake levels within East
Africa, matching the succession in the Chad Basin, was first established by Butzer et al. (1972) on the basis of the available

3. For the Second Cataract reaches of Nubia, W. Adams
(1965) argues for increasing Nile floods of destructive proportions early in the Christian era. By A.D. 450, the village of
Meinarti began to serve as a center of agglomeration for smaller
settlements abandoned on the floodplain. Then, from ca. A.D.
600-1000, Meinarti itself was repeatedly ravaged by high floods,
until flood volumes apparently declined once again in the
eleventh century. The reasons for resettlement may have been
complex, however. Arminna West, further north in Egyptian Nubia,
was prosperous throughout this period, despite its riverbank location (Trigger 1970). The basic similarities between the
evidence from Aksha and Meinarti suggest that the location of
the latter site, within a very constricted part of the valley,
made it unusually susceptible--and sensitive--to Nile vari-
ation. In Egypt proper, semicontinuous gauge readings are available from the El-Roda Nilometer at Cairo, since A.D. 622 (Popper
1951), and accurate records of Nile volume at Aswan since A.D.
1869 are reported by Hurst and Phillips (1936, pp. 30 ff.). A
much-needed, systematic evaluation of these historical records
is under way by Barbara Bell.

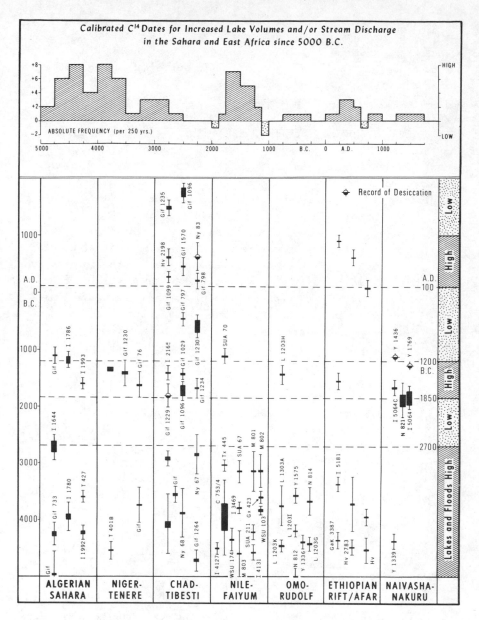

Fig. 5.--Corrected radiocarbon dates for increased lake volume or stream discharge in East Africa and the southern Sahara. Calibration after Ralph, Michael, and Han (1973). Brackets indicate 2σ margins. Note that some laboratory numbers remain unpublished.

radiocarbon dates.

   It is now possible to examine the available evidence for
greater lake volumes or stream discharge in more detail, for the
period since 5000 B.C., and to extend the survey area to the central and southern Sahara as well as eastern and northeastern
Africa. Figure 5 has been assembled for this purpose, utilizing
a wide range of additional or newer sources, including Faure (1966),
Conrad (1969), Servant, Servant, and Délibrias (1969), Williams
and Adamson (1974), and Gasse, Fontes, and Rognon (1974). The
dates shown in figure 5 include all assays on materials relevant
to demonstrated positive or negative hydrological trends. They
are plotted with their 2σ margins and, wherever available, their
laboratory numbers. They are, furthermore, calibrated to calendar
years as closely as is now possible (see Ralph, Michael, and Han
1973). However, systematic errors of calibration remain (Burleigh,
Switsur, and Renfrew 1973), and a percentage of chronometric assays
are inherently inaccurate. Consequently only the overall picture
is valid, as a composite, and the temporal boundaries between wet
and dry intervals shown on figure 5 are necessarily approximate.
The frequency histogram at the top of figure 5, recording the
number of dates for high or low lakes (or stream discharge) in
units of 250 years, summarizes the chronometric results.[4]

   Surprising is the degree of concordance, and the broad
parallelism of long-term trends throughout the area considered.
An attenuated but fluctuating moist interval began prior to 5000
B.C. and came to an end ca. 2700 ± 100 B.C. The frequency histogram suggests that three submaxima were centered at about 4500,
3750, and 3000 B.C. Lake levels and stream discharge were severely
reduced after 2700 B.C., and a slight apparent overlap of positive
and negative records argues for wetter conditions beginning 1850

---

   4. For an outline of the substantial geological evidence,
and information on the amplitude of lake level fluctuations,
see the original sources quoted above. Of particular relevance
to the Nile Basin are the changes of Lake Rudolf, which began to
rise from about its present level some 6,600 years ago and
reached a high level of +65-+70 m about 5000 B.C. (see Butzer,
Isaac, et al. 1972). This level, which represents a lake volume
almost three times that of today, persisted with fluctuations
until a little after 2900 B.C. It was followed by a regression
of unknown amplitude and then by a final transgression to +70 m
a little before 1500 B.C. Similar events, including a number of
dated, minor fluctuations during the last three millennia, can
be cited from the smaller lakes of the central Ethiopian Rift
and Afar.

± 50 B.C. This second moist interlude was relatively brief, but
marked by greatly expanded lakes throughout the area: Lake
Rudolf was 70 m deeper and overflowed into the Nile drainage
(Butzer, Brown, and Thurber 1969), while the White Nile flowed some
2-3 m higher than the modern river, with a discharge estimated,
on the basis of channel island morphology, to be ten times greater
(Berry 1960; Williams and Adamson 1974). The termination of
this wet phase is again conveniently marked by a slight, apparent
overlap of dates for high Saharan lakes and for the sudden and
total desiccation of Lake Naivasha. The best available approximation is 1200 ± 50 B.C. Later moist intervals were relatively un-
important, and are limited to the Chad Basin or the Ethiopian
lowlands. Confirmation from both areas is limited to the first
millennium A.D. (ca. 100-1000 ± 75 A.D.), a time when Lake Rudolf
was 25-35 m higher than at present (Butzer 1971b, pp. 93 ff.,
130).

      This comparative material greatly strengthens Bell's overall
interpretation of the Nile flood record, while providing a more
general perspective. There clearly was a significant decline of
Nile discharge, in the order of 30% or more, after the 1st Dynasty.
Floods remained generally lower during the Old Kingdom, until
well into the Middle Kingdom. Within this setting, repeated failure of the floods during the First Intermediate Period must be
rated as a relatively short-term anomaly, analogous to desiccation
along the southern Sahara margins in the 1970s. These relatively
brief but disastrous events appear to mark the climax of some
eight centuries of drier climate in tropical Africa. Subsequently,
the abnormally high floods of ca. 1840-1770 B.C. seem to have
ushered in a new era of improved hydrological conditions, and
their dimensions find an important confirmation in the central
Sudan. After some six or seven centuries this era of a munificient
Nile drew to an end, rather abruptly, probably during the reign
of Ramses III (1182-1151 B.C.) (see pp. 55-56). Thereafter conditions fluctuated closer to the modern mean, with secular trends of
a few centuries' duration favoring moderately lower or higher Niles.

Changing Floodplain Topography

      In closing this discussion of the Dynastic evolution of the
Nile floodplain, it remains to consider the former topography
of the river and its distributary channels. There are no direct
data to this effect. Geo-archeological trenches were cut and

studied by Vermeersch (1970) at El-Kab, where they elucidated
the early Holocene history of the modern floodplain. Such studies
are urgently required in other, critical valley sectors. Meanwhile
we are restricted to a record of historical cartography that only
begins in 1799 (Jacotin 1826), to the second-century writings
of Claudius Ptolemy (Ball 1942, pp. 85-130), to a reevaluation
of the borings published by Attia (1954), and to a complex floodplain morphology represented on modern topographic maps and visible
from satellite photography. For this purpose an intensive pilot
study was undertaken of a 70-km stretch of the valley north of
Sohag. The results properly belong with an extended paper in
preparation for the Hellenistic and Islamic periods, but the interim
conclusions can be usefully summarized here.

    The French survey of 1799-1800, done at a scale of 1:100,000
(Jacotin 1826), is detailed but inaccurate. Ball (1932) has shown
that the areal and linear distortion as well as incorrect orien-
tations are a result of far too few or even faulty astronomical
observations for basic coordinates. However, the Nile channel
and that of other key canals and branches can be reliably "un-
scrambled" by reference to village sites and contemporary topographic features. The significant shifts of channel islands,
talwegs, and so on, can be verified by the so-called irrigation
map of Egypt, surveyed 1870-71 (Ball 1932), reproduced for the
Sohag sector by Willcocks (1904, plan 14). These maps show positions of the Nile intermediate between those of 1800 and 1935.
Finally, the substantial changes near Qaw el-Kebir are historical-
ly documented in Brunton (1927, p. 3, pl. 1). The import of these
channel shifts is a notable reduction of channel sinuosity from
1.33 in 1800 to 1.25 in 1935, this trend continuing on recent
survey revisions. This straightening out of the Nile channel
may reflect both a decline of Nile volume and increasing "sediment starvation" due to the impoundment of water behind barrages
and dams. The maximum change was a 1.5-km talweg shift near Qaw.

    By mapping the abandoned levees and channel traces, in part
corroborated by anomalous administrative boundaries, the state
of the river in 1800 allows a projection of the channel for the
seventeenth century A.D., assuming a constant rate of change.
The channel so reconstructed for the early 1600s has a sinuosity
of 1.36 and shows talweg shifts of as much as 2.3 km from those
of today. Altogether, of seventeen deviations documented, eleven
have involved eastward migrations of the Nile channel. The same

selective eastward shift is apparent from the preferential location of multiple abandoned levees now as much as 5.5 km west
of their functional counterparts.

A net eastward movement of the Nile over the last two millennia is implicitly documented by Ptolemy, who lists El-Manshah
(Psoi) and Akhmim (Khant-Min) in similar positions on the river,
but Qaw (Djuka) away from the river to the east, Kom Ishqaw
(Edjoet) away from the river to the west (for locations and ancient
names see fig. 11 and table 2).[5] This argues that the Nile flowed past Akhmim to run immediately west of a series of prominent
levees at El-Maragha, Tahta, and Tima in Hellenistic times. This
course was on the average at least 3 km west of the modern Nile.

Reconstruction of the suballuvial geology from well logs
and bore profiles (see Attia 1954, pp. 45-52), as attempted in
figure 1, verifies this eastward trend and suggests that when the
modern alluvium began to accumulate in Old Kingdom times, the
Nile axis ran from Sohag to Tahta, rejoining the modern channel
near Abutig. The combination of surface topography and borings
also verifies that an ancestor of the Sohagiya Canal has been
meandering across the eastern half of the floodplain not only
since the Old Kingdom, but also in terminal Pleistocene or early
Holocene times (see fig. 1).

Extrapolating these realizations to the length of the Egyptian Nile Valley, examination of further sample sections in key
areas between Luxor and Beni Suef shows that the course of the
Nile was substantially different in Dynastic times, with the degree of sinuosity variable in response to long-term fluctuations
of volume. This means that meander location as well as amplitude
and wavelength have been subject to repeated change, changes that
are impossible to reconstruct with the available information.
However, the axis of the Nile ran far west of its present course
between Akhmim and Cairo, past such ancient cities as El-Qusiya
(Kos) and El-Ashmunein (Khmun), with El-Qeis (Sako) and Memphis
(Menfe) still on the river in Ptolemy's day (see figs. 4 and 11).
Relatively minor modifications are apparent in the constricted
valley farther south.

5. See Ball (1942, p. 112), but note that Ball's reconstructions of the Nile (his fig. 17 and pl. 2) are inconsonant
with Ptolemy's description.

The implications for the northern half of the valley are
momentous: the economic base for east-bank towns along this sector has changed dramatically and the actual settlement sites corresponding to many cemeteries now preserved on the eastern desert
edge must have been destroyed by the river. In fact, many of the
settlement problems posed by this part of Egypt, as discussed
further below, reflect on these fundamental geographical changes.

Changes in the Delta and Faiyum

The vicissitudes of climate in East Africa and high lati-
tudes were not without impact in the northern Delta. Here the
coastal sector had confronted higher world sea levels of +2 m or
more ca. 3000 B.C. and again ca. 1200 B.C., as well as lower sea
levels of -2 m or so ca. 2200 B.C. and again 300 B.C. (see
Hafemann 1960; Lind 1969; Butzer 1975b; Larsen 1975). Although
related transgressive sediments in the Delta now lie below the
modern 1-m contour, due to autocompaction, the subsurface geology
shows that coastal lagoons did not generally extend south of the
present 2-m contour at any time during the deposition of the
recent Nile mud (fig. 4). Marine transgressions were apparently
offset by the accelerated alluviation and higher Nile floods during
the 1st Dynasty and again in the ninth and seventh centuries B.C.
These served to raise the level of the natural levees, adding
more sediment to the coast. Littoral inundation was evidently
limited, with no "backflooding" in the southern delta. Basically modern coastal features are apparent from Strabo's description of ca. 25 B.C. (see Ball 1942, pp. 57 ff.) and, near the
easternmost, Pelusiac Mouth, had begun to form during the first
century A.D. (Sneh and Weissbrod 1973).

In the Faiyum, too, the level of Lake Moeris--the an-
cestral Birket Qarun--fluctuated according to the season and
strength of the Nile floods. Probable quays on the northwestern
shoreline at Qasr es-Sagha and Dimeh, related to nearby Old
Kingdom quarries, are at 18-22 m absolute elevation (Ball 1939,
p. 215; Kees 1961, p. 223; Said, Albritton, et al. 1972). Although there is no direct information on the antiquity of the
Bahr Yusef (Butzer 1973), the Hawara channel across the Nile-
Faiyum divide may have silted up during the low floods of the
First Intermediate Period, cutting off much of the water supply (Ball 1939, pp. 199 ff.; Bell 1971, 1975), either until the
12th-Dynasty pharaoh Amenemhet I (1991-1962 B.C.) cleared the

Bahr Yusef channel between Hawara and Lahun, or until the pheno-
menal floods after 1840 B.C. cleared it hydrodynamically. However, the colossi of Biyahmu (courtyard pavement at 18 m, Ball
1939, p. 206; Bell 1975) infer a mean low level for Lake Moeris
below 18 m at the time of Amenemhet III (modern annual lake amplitude is 0.6-1.2 m, and would be 3 m or more without artificial
controls, see Ball 1939, p. 234). More likely is a lake level
somewhat below +15 m, to allow for emergence of and access to the
Thermutis Temple at Madinet Madi (see Vogliano 1936, fig. 1).[6]
This potentially allows for a minimum of 275 sq km and possibly as
much as 450 sq km of cultivable ground in the Twelfth Dynasty,
below a waterhead of 24 m.

The lake may again have been above 25 m when Herodotus (II:
149) appears to have found the colossi of Biyahmu partially submerged (Bell 1975), and claimed an outflow of water to the Nile
Valley during the low water season--a reasonable probability since
the level of a low Nile adjacent to the Faiyum entrance, at
Beni Suef, is even now only 18 m. It remains a moot point whether
the level of Lake Moeris fell 25 m or more during the century
after Herodotus, or whether the early Ptolemies (particularly
II, Philadelphus, 285-246 B.C.) artificially lowered the lakes
to -2 m (Ball 1939, pp. 210 ff.) or -13 m and below (Caton-
Thompson and Gardner 1929; Caton-Thompson, Gardner, and Huzayyin
1937). The lower end of a canal system of Ptolemy II on the
northern edge of the Faiyum implies a lake level certainly below
-5 m (Caton-Thompson and Gardner 1934, p. 144) ca. 265 B.C., and
to obtain an appreciable amount of emergent land in the northern
Faiyum, lake level would indeed need to be below -13 m. With a
closed lock at Hawara and the prevailing open-water evaporation
rate of 5.5 mm per day (2 m per year), the level of Lake Moeris
could be artificially lowered a full 38 m in about twenty years,
making allowance for some lake influx from groundwater seepage.
Allowing some water passage at Hawara to maintain basic irrigation, the same effect could be achieved in forty years. Since
it is unlikely in terms of the East African paleohydrologic
record that Nile floods were high in the fourth century B.C.,
Lake Moeris was probably well down from its fifth-century level.

6.   The base of the Kom is at 15-16 m (see Army Map Service,
Washington, D.C., sheet 5483, 1:100,000 series P 677, compiled
1959).

However, a substantial and rapid reduction of the lake was within the technological capacity of the early Ptolemies.

5

ENVIRONMENT AND TECHNOLOGY IN DYNASTIC TIMES

The preceding discussion shows to what degree the environmental history and controls of Dynastic Egypt are now better understood than those of any other region over a comparable span
of time. The ecological system was not stable, and clearly required repeated adjustments. At the same time, the Valley floodplain, the Delta, and the Faiyum provided somewhat different sets
of opportunities. Against this background it is now possible to
review the potential impacts of environmental change, and above
all to examine the role of technology and organizational skills
in overcoming ecological problems and in developing the cultural
landscape.

The Desert Frontiers

*Rainfall in Egypt proper became a rare event following the
close of the Predynastic moist interval, ca. 2900 B.C., and even
more so by the beginning of the Middle Kingdom, ca. 2040 B.C.

To what extent were these changes in the desert ecology of
Egypt significant in human terms? After all, Predynastic desert
rains did not provide more than a slight amelioration of the
prevailing aridity. Logically, however, the almost total failure of rains south of the latitude of Memphis by the time of the
Middle Kingdom would have reduced the resources and numbers of the
desert nomads. It would also have rendered travel between the
Nile and the Red Sea, or between the Libyan oases and the Nile,
far more difficult, while eliminating seasonal pastoral activities by valley folk out onto the desert. The abandonment of late
Predynastic desert-margin settlements near or at Hierakonpolis,
Armant, Nagada South Town, Abydos, and Mahasna (see Butzer 1959c)
may therefore be causally related.

Equally so, one cannot escape the potential relevance of the climatic events of the First Intermediate Period for desert dwellers west and east of the Egyptian and Nubian Nile. The abandonment of several oases in the Southern Libyan Desert, for example, Dungul at some time after ca. 2050 ± 180 B.C. (see Hobler and Hester 1969), presumably was symptomatic of this trend. Particularly relevant was the large-scale settlement of Lower Nubia by the C-Group people from the (?southern) Libyan Desert (Bietak 1968, pp. 141 ff.). The earliest settlements, suggesting a seminomadic subsistence, date from the closing years of the 6th Dynasty and are significantly restricted to the west bank of the Nile in central Lower Nubia. By the end of the First Intermediate Period the C-Group people had spread northward to beyond Aswan, and occupied both sides of the valley as far south as Wadi Halfa. Nomadic pressures of the Libyan Tjemehu (who may or may not be related to the C-Group people, see Bietak 1968, p. 147; Zibelius 1972, pp. 184 ff.) continued along the west bank of the river, and such nomads were conscripted to work on the temple of Wadi Sebua in the time of Ramses II. It is therefore possible that the many Egyptian administrative attempts in the major Libyan oases (Bahariya, Farafra, Kharga, Dakhla) since the 6th Dynasty (Fakhry 1974b) were intended not only to protect the desert trade routes but also to forestall encroachment by desert groups; a systematic analysis of the literary and archeological materials might shed further light on this frontier. Egyptian punitive raids against the pastoral Libyans of the coastal steppe west of the Delta apparently were commonplace in Old Kingdom times, and Libyan attacks and infiltration were almost incessant from the death of Ramses II until a Libyan dynasty was established in the Delta and Faiyum about 945 B.C. (Černý 1965).

This brief excursion into the history of the western frontiers shows that the failure of the rains was of indirect significance for Egypt. Furthermore, it is possible that Egyptian access to the mineral resources of the Eastern Desert and Sinai was also conditioned on ecological stress affecting the indigenous nomads.[1] In other words, although the geographical isolation of

1. Nomadic pressures from the eastern desert are first recorded in 12th-Dynasty times. A substantial infiltration of the Pan-Grave people, or Medja, from the Red Sea Hills began after 1800 B.C. and continued for almost three centuries (Bietak 1968, pp. 149 ff.). Akin to the modern Beja, these folk settled primarily along the eastern margins of the Nile in Lower Nubia.

the Nile oasis was enhanced, the social conflicts of the Red and
the Black Land, the desert and the alluvium, were not eliminated
but probably intensified. More research on these issues is urgently required.

The Nature of Irrigation Agriculture

The ecological impact of long-term diminutions of Nile
floods after 2900 B.C. or 1200 B.C., the excessive floods of the
late Middle Kingdom, or the short-term Nile failures of the First
Intermediate Period and early Middle Kingdom will have been direct and momentous. In general, the Nile flood regime is more
predictable and reliable than that of any other world river,
thanks to the multiplicity of its water sources in sub-Saharan
Africa, and the basic regularity of the monsoonal rains. Yet, as
we have seen, both the measurements of Nile flood level or volume
since A.D. 622 and the historical record of Nile floods show a
substantial degree of short- and long-term variability: good,
mediocre, and poor floods; periodic floods either excessive or
grossly deficient; and trends that over decades or centuries spell
improving or declining resources. On a year-to-year basis, the
food supply and tax yield were inevitably affected, since adequate
but not excessive flood level and sufficiently persistent inundation are prerequisites to both natural and artificial irrigation.
On a decade-to-decade basis, periodic low or abnormally high
floods exceeded the competence of irrigation technology, to bring
crop failures or catastrophic levee breaches, with attendant famine
and loss of life. Over decades and centuries, trends to lower
or higher floods led to modifications of river channels, levees,
and flood basins, threatening the efficacy of the total irrigation system, and possibly subjecting the economic and political
structure of the country to intolerable stress.

As in recent years, the fundamental response of strong central governments to the perennial vagaries of the Nile would
presumably have entailed repeated elaborations of the system of
artificial irrigation. This role of government is documented in
the development of the Faiyum under the early Ptolemies (Caton-
Thompson and Gardner 1929; Crawford 1971). It is also implied
by the extensive architectural activities of the 12th-Dynasty
pharaohs near the Nile-Faiyum divide (see Porter and Moss 1934,
pp. 96 ff.; Ball 1939, p. 104; Simpson 1963). However, Dynastic
records , compared with those of the Hellenistic period, are la-

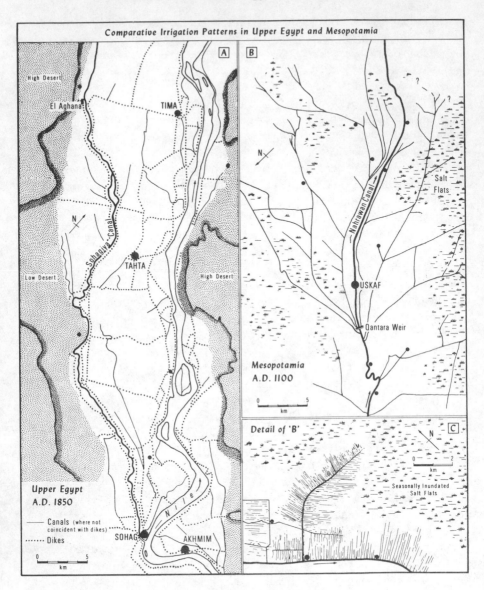

Fig. 6.--Comparative irrigation networks in Upper Egypt and Mesopotamia. *A*, example of linear, basin irrigation in Sohag province,
ca. A.D. 1850. *B*, example of radial canalization system in the
lower Nahrawan region, southeast of Baghdad; Abbasid (A.D. 883-
1150). Modified after R.M. Adams (1965, fig. 9). Same scale as
Egyptian counterpart. *C*, detail of field canal layout in figure
6,*B*. Simplified after R.M. Adams (1965, fig. 10).

mentably uninformative regarding irrigation technology, water legislation, labor deployment, and related administrative procedures.
Klaus Baer (in preparation) explains this by a relatively decentralized system of basin irrigation, with regulation essentially
a local matter. Such a view finds considerable, if indirect,
support. One factor is that natural irrigation of the Nile's
flood basins (fig. 6,A) would render complex but shallow, radial
canal networks of the Faiyum or Mesopotamian type, for example
as documented for Khuzistan (Neely 1974), the Diyala Plains (R.
Adams 1965), and the Uruk area (Adams and Nissen 1972) (figs.
6,B and 6,C), impractical if not superfluous. Another is that
the necessary technology for large-scale perennial irrigation was
unavailable until the nineteenth century A.D., when the traditional, basin or paleotechnic system (Hamdan 1961) began to come

Fig. 7.--Abandoned
shaduf and irrigation
ditch, on Nile bank
at Kalabsha West.
Photograph by the
author (January 1963).

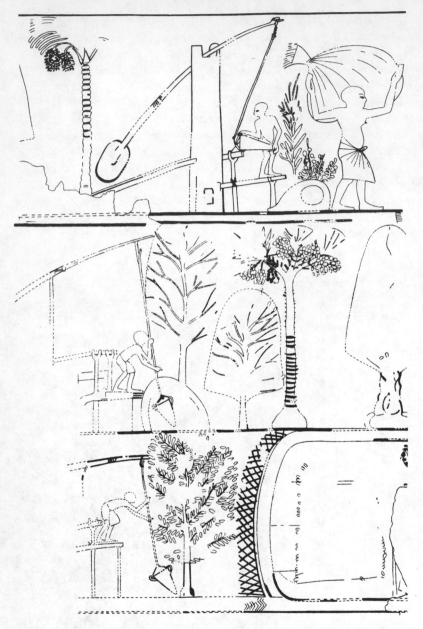

Fig. 8.--Shadufs of the Amarna period, from the tomb of Nefer-Hotep at Thebes. Note irrigation of date palms and other orchard trees, and the apparent tank or pool (lower right). The water pattern in lowest margin suggests lifting out of an irrigation canal. From Davies (1933, pl. 46 and 47). (The Metropolitan Museum of Art, drawing by Egyptian Expedition)

Fig. 9.--Cow-drawn saqiya, with old wheel in foreground, irriga-
ting date palm grove at Hierakonpolis. Photograph by the author
(February 1958).

to an end.

Apart from the representation of the Scorpion King breach-
ing a levee or dike (fig. 2), there is an unambiguous allusion to
Pepi I (ca. 2390-2360 B.C.) cutting a canal to place a tract of
land under water (Sethe 1933, § 220-21, translated in Dunham 1938).
Equally significant, however, is the indirect evidence of cut-
stone revetments, large piers, and extensive, artificial basins
on the desert edge between Giza and Abu Sir (Goyon 1971; also
Kemp and O'Connor 1974). These harbor installations are linked
to the valley temples or, by rock-cut ramps, to the nearby pyramids of Khufu (ca. 2606-2583 B.C.), Khafre (ca. 2575-2550 B.C.),
Menkaure (ca. 2548-2530 B.C.), Unas (ca. 2430-2400 B.C.), and
Pepi II (ca. 2355-2261 B.C.). Beyond any subsequent mortuary,
ceremonial role, they must originally have served in the large-
scale transport and unloading of building stone. Contrary to
a widespread belief, the general depth of flood water (less than
1.5 m) on cultivated fields near Cairo is insufficient for systematic navigation by heavily loaded barges, quite apart from
the fact that the flood surge has a duration of only four to
six weeks. Whether or not there was a secondary or tertiary Nile

branch running along the western desert edge,[2] major transfers
of limestone blocks *across* the floodplain from the quarries on
the eastern side of the valley can only have been reasonably
achieved by a large, transverse canal. This, together with
other vague suggestions of canal digging and basin creation from
the Old Kingdom (Sethe 1933, § 212; also Westermann 1919), argues
for rudimentary artificial irrigation well prior to the First
Intermediate Period (contra Schenkel 1974).

Water lifting in Old Kingdom times was limited to manual
transport of buckets, shown attached to a shoulder yoke in Middle
Kingdom tomb frescoes. Only in the Amarna period (ca. 1346-
1334 B.C.) (see Giles 1970, pp. 91 ff.) is the shaduf or pole-
and-bucket lever (fig. 7), singly capable of raising containers
of water well over 1 m, verified by the representational art
(see Davies 1903, p. 41, pl. 32; Davies 1933, pp. 36, 70 ff.;
contra Winlock 1947, pp. 165 f.) (fig. 8). The animal-drawn
waterwheel or saqiya (fig. 9), able to lift a fairly substantial
quantity of water--almost continuously--to elevations in excess
of 3.5 m, was only introduced to Egypt in Persian or Ptolemaic
times (Schnebel 1925, pp. 73 ff.; Caton-Thompson and Gardner
1934, p. 150; Ball 1939, pp. 210 f.; Crawford 1971, p. 107). It
did not reach Nubia until the beginning of the Christian era
(Adams 1975). Although the technology to excavate navigation
canals already existed in the Old Kingdom (see Kemp and O'Connor
1974), modern experiences with deep irrigation canals, cut to

2. Goyon (1971) argues for an elaborate canal network, in
Old Kingdom times, linking the Giza pyramids to an extension of
the Bahr Yusef in the south and northward, along the western margin of the Delta, into the Maryut. Although it is quite possible
that a minor Nile branch did exist between the Faiyum entrance
and the apex of the Delta, Goyon's west-delta canal is based on
speculative deductions. It is also superfluous from the perspective of navigation or irrigation, quite apart from the stupendous
technical problems to such a project at that time. For the
northeasternmost Delta, Sneh, Weissbrod, and Perath (1975) interpret two segments of abandoned canal between Sile (El-Qantara)
and the classical Pelusiac Mouth as the lower end of a great
"Eastern Canal" linked up to the Nile via the Wadi Tumilat, favoring a Middle Kingdom age (on some quite tenuous argumentation).
This very obvious feature on the air photographs had a water
level width of 70 m (compared with 54 m for the Suez Canal of
A.D. 1871). It is important to note that (1) archeological examination has not been carried out; (2) the obvious head of this
canal was the Pelusiac branch near Kom Dafana (at a time when the
lower Pelusiac branch did not yet exist), not the distant Wadi
Tumilat; and (3) a defensive and irrigation canal in this area
would certainly postdate the Hyksos and presumably be Ramessid.

riverbed level, show that they silt up almost immediately (Crouchley 1938, pp. 54 ff.).

On the other hand, the gentle longitudinal gradient of the
Nile (1:12,000) is unsuitable for radial canalization below a
high waterhead, such as in the case of the Mesopotamian counterpart (fig. 6). The only exception to this is the Faiyum, where
complex canalization was first put into operation under the
Ptolemies. In particular, control sluices were constructed in
the Nile-Faiyum exit at Lahun, feeding a radial system of relatively high-gradient canals and keeping the level of Lake Moeris
well below -5 m (Strabo xvii:1.37; Ball 1939, pp. 212 f.; Caton-
Thompson and Gardner 1929, 1934, pp. 140 ff., 156 f.; Crawford
1971, p. 41, with references). This simultaneous operation of
irrigation and reclamation trebled the cultivable land of the
Faiyum to a maximum of 1,300 sq km, a figure similar to that of
A.D. 1882, compared with about 1,800 sq km today. But on the
Nile floodplain and delta, true canal irrigation was unknown until A.D. 1843, when a system of barrages began to provide the
necessary waterhead for extended, arterial feeder canals.

In other words, Dynastic irrigation technology was severely
circumscribed by a lack of suitable mechanical lifting devices
as well as by the impossibility of implementing low-water canalization (contra Schenkel 1973, 1974). The technology was instead geared primarily toward regulation of the high-water Nile:
conversion of the natural to higher and stronger artificial levees;
enlarging and dredging of natural diverging overflow channels;
blocking off of natural, gathering or drainage channels by earthen
dams and sluice gates; subdivision of the flood basins by dams
into manageable, in part special-purpose, units; and control-
ling water access to and retention in the basin subunits by temporary cuts in the levees or dikes or by a network of short
canals and masonry gates.

Since manual or shaduf lifting is only practicable in a local,
horticultural context, it is not surprising that there are no
Dynastic records of summer crops planted after the harvest of
winter wheat, barley, and flax (see Helck 1960-64, pp. 754 ff.).
Nor, as Baer (1962, 1963) has carefully demonstrated, is there
evidence for flood season crops being grown during the inundation
on high ground that required irrigation water, or on low lands
protected from flooding.

Schenkel (1973) argues for an increasing frequency of summer irrigation in New Kingdom and Ptolemaic times, based on interpretation of the terms $ḥrw$ and $q̣3jt$ as low and high fields, respectively, with $ḥrw$ further subdivided into categories of old (tnj) and fresh ($nḥb$) soil (?) (on these basic dichotomies see also Gardiner 1948, pp. 27 ff., 178 ff.; Helck 1960-64, pp. 290 ff.). Schenkel further deduces that the $q̣3jt$ were normal basin lands with a single irrigated crop, whereas the $ḥrw$ were inundated even during low floods, and allowed summer irrigation, with $nḥb$ yielding two good crops, tnj two mediocre crops per year. The interpretation of these field categories is to some degree a matter of etymological guesswork,[3] and, as refined by Schenkel, is largely based on a misconception of floodplain morphology. In particular, Schenkel (1973) claims that Helck's (1963, pp. 298 ff.) areal reconstructions of field and village layouts for northern Middle Egypt in Papyrus Wilbour (ca. 1141 B.C.) show a preponderance of $nḥb$ and tnj holdings in immediate Nile proximity and at the Faiyum entrance, with most $q̣3jt$ further out, often near the desert margins. In fact, as has been outlined above, and as is also apparent from the topographic maps, the lowest floodplain segments are not in channel proximity but near the basin centers or even at the very edge of the desert. Schenkel's tenuous argument is therefore unacceptable. Altogether, the intricate, checkerboard patterns of interwoven, irrigated, derelict (fallow, flooded, saline, or unirrigated), and waterlogged fields documented for the Ptolemaic Faiyum by Crawford (1971, chap. 7, pp. 160 f.) caution against simplistic and unwarranted assumptions from the relatively vague literary record of the Dynastic period.

The elaborate modern system of winter, summer, and flood crops characteristic of perennial irrigation could only begin to evolve after introduction of the saqiya or after inauguration of a successful, high-waterhead canal system. Both these prerequisites were first met in the Ptolemaic Faiyum, and it is therefore not surprising that complex cropping is first verified there in the third century B.C. (see Crawford 1971, pp. 112 ff.).

3. Klaus Baer: personal communication.

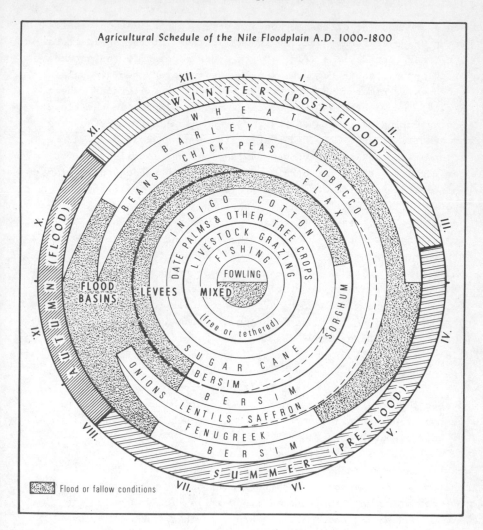

Fig. 10.--Circular agricultural schedule for the Nile floodplain,
A.D. 1000-1800. Data based on Niemeyer (1936).

     Even so, the dominant crops and the agricultural cycle were
significantly different in Ptolemaic, let alone Dynastic, times
(see Helck 1960-64, pp. 754 ff.), compared with those of today.
Niemeyer (1936, pp. 54 ff., tables 1 and 2), based primarily on
the *Déscription de l'Égypte*, has carefully reconstructed the agricultural patterns of the eighteenth century--prior to the large-

scale development of cash crops and perennial irrigation. Utilizing Niemeyer's raw data, an annual schedule of the agricultural
cycle has been devised (fig. 10) in order to clarify the nature
of the crops, their temporal sequences, and preferred floodplain
ecozones. Primary subsistence was based on cereal grains (wheat,
barley) and vegetables (beans, chick peas), planted in the flood
basins during early winter together with flax, a primary source
of textile fiber. Provided that irrigation was available, a
second flood basin crop of vegetables (onions, lentils) and fodder (Egyptian clover or bersim, fenugreek) was subsequently planted
in summer, the latter helping to regenerate soil fertility and
providing livestock feed. The levees and their higher-lying
backslopes were reserved for date palm groves, cultivation of
sugar cane and cotton throughout the year, and a summer crop sequence of sorghum followed by bersim. Except for the deep-rooted
palms, these cultures required intensive irrigation of the high
levees. Significantly, sugar, cotton, and rice (mainly in the
Delta) were only introduced early in the Islamic period, while
sorghum is not verified until Greek or Roman-Byzantine times
(Cadell 1970; Dixon 1969; Crawford 1971, pp. 112 ff.; Hamdan
1961; Niemeyer 1936, pp. 61 ff.). In other words, Egypt lacked
its cash crops and its key summer cereal as late as the Ptolemaic
era. It also lacked its critical levee crops, thus obviating
a need for more than incidental summer irrigation of garden plots,
such as those detailed on the Scorpion mace-head or the reliefs
of Deir el-Bahari (ca. 1490 B.C.) (Naville 1906, pl. 142).

All of the information that can be brought to bear on Dynastic land use in Egypt shows a simple pattern of winter agriculture, largely confined to the flood basins, with their crude
but effective system of annual flood irrigation. Despite the
symbolic association of the pharaoh with this inundation, Dynastic irrigation technology was rudimentary and operated at a
local rather than a national scale (see also J.A. Wilson in
Kraeling and Adams 1960, p. 128). Perhaps the only centralized
aspect was the traditional link between tax rates and the potential harvest, as inferred from the height of each Nile flood.
Yet even the standard Nilometers used for this purpose were
situated at different points along the Nile (see Borchardt 1934).
Altogether it seems that, away from the major urban hinterlands
and the key royal domains, no form of centralized canal network
was ever achieved in Dynastic times. In this same light the

development of the Delta during and after the Old Kingdom (Butzer 1974), or the Faiyum projects undertaken by Amenemhet III
and Ptolemy II (Crawford 1971, pp. 40 ff.), should only be viewed
as examples of state efforts to develop unproductive, marginal
lands for purposes of revenue (Kemp 1972a), to support or re-
ward civil and military officials (Smith 1972), or to settle
veterans and mercenaries (O'Connor 1972a). Dynastic irrigation
was naturally compartmentalized, so that a centralized administration was neither practicable nor purposeful. This rudimentary
form of artificial irrigation was also limited in its scope.
Apart from restricted, perennial application to home or market
gardens, it was designed to amplify the acreage and yield of
winter crops, to reduce the effects of year-to-year flood variability, and to protect settlements and fields from flood damage.
It was nonetheless inadequate to cope with excessive or deficient
floods, or with long-term trends of decreasing flood volume.

The Impact of Very High or Low Floods

Excessive floods, such as those of A.D. 1818-19, were an
occasion of terror and massive rallying of the rural populace, as
graphically described by Willcocks (1904, p. 71). They tended
to destroy the transverse dikes that subdivided basins and to
raze settlement sites, destroying food stores, endangering seed
stocks for the next planting season, and decimating livestock.
Continuous artificial levees adequate to control such floods
were unavailable in Herodotus' day (II:94, 97) or even in the early
nineteenth century A.D. The only alternative solution would
have been to raise dikes around settlements and temple storage
complexes (see Herodotus II:99), and to remove herd animals to
the desert margins before it was too late. Water did in fact
break into the temple precincts at Karnak during very high floods
(see Habachi 1974).[4] Exceptionally long periods of flooding
significantly reduced crop yields by favoring plant parasites in
the soil and by delaying harvest until April, when the hot kham-
sin winds might parch the crop (Willcocks and Craig 1913, p. 304).
Considerable labor would also have been required to render canals and embankments operational again.

4. In the fourth year of the reign of Sobekhotep VII, ca.
1680 B.C., we read that the temple hall was flooded and that the
pharaoh went wading in it together with the workmen.

Such measures presumably were within the capacity of 12th-
Dynasty pharaohs such as Amenemhet III and, when properly anti-
cipated, exceptionally high floods such as those of 1840-1770
B.C. should have proved less deleterious than deficient ones.
Bell (1975) suggests that some form of adjustment was achieved,
only to have a return to more normal conditions later in the
13th Dynasty (ca. 1784-1668 B.C.) lead to renewed hardship.
This seems somewhat unlikely, and the economic decline of 13th-
Dynasty Egypt at a time of maximum Nile discharge (ca. 1850-1200
B.C.) may just as well have been influenced by continuingly erratic
Nile behavior for which we generally lack written records.[5]   In
all probability, a long-term trend to higher floods would entail
several centuries of natural readjustment--including a higher-
lying, broader, and sandier channel; higher and more massive banks,
additionally buttressed by artificial embankments; increased discharge and channel mobility in a distributary such as the Bahr
Yusef; and lateral erosion of valley margin dunes or flooding of
intradunal swales, so as to expand the alluvial plain. Once a
new steady state was established, the agricultural resource base
would be considerably greater than before, as well as increasingly stable. This state of readjustment may have been completed
in Egypt by the late Hyksos era (ca. 1668-1560 B.C.).[6]

Floods with unusually low or brief crests implied that substantial segments of the floodplain would have remained dry, in-
sufficiently wetted, or devoid of an increment of fresh, fertile
sediment. Although plots appear to have been highly fragmented
(Baer 1963; Helck 1960-64, pp. 298 ff.) and therefore scattered,
so protecting the major landholders, individual tenants would

5. See, for example, the high flood recorded for Sobekhotep
VII (Habachi 1974).

6. The architectural record of riverbank sites from the Old
and Middle kingdoms is comparatively scanty and has so far yield-
ed no geo-archeological insights as to flood damage or floodplain
changes. In the case of the New Kingdom, numerous temple sites
seem to have been placed with respect to a floodplain approximately
similar to that of today. But no meaningful conclusions are
warranted without at least several detailed studies of founda-
tion contacts (seldom accessible to any but the excavators, who
have habitually ignored such potential information) or of silt
lapping up against or over pediments, retaining walls, and so
on (mainly removed in the nineteenth century, without any record).

potentially be hard hit wherever water was inadequate. So, for
example, the poor flood of A.D. 1877 was only 2 m below average, but it left 35% of the Nile Valley unirrigated (see Willcocks and Craig 1913, table 176), including 62% of Qena and 75%
of Girga province, where perennial irrigation was not yet effective. It can hardly be overemphasized that a Nile failure of
serious proportions would lead to widespread starvation, wholesale
destruction of livestock, and pressure on essential seed stocks.
If continued over several years, marginal lands would be abandoned, with attendant social problems in areas of relocation, and
soaring mortality that would affect the demographic structure
selectively. Under extreme circumstances, no foresight in centers
of administration could cushion the impact of the proverbial
seven lean years. Total economic disruption and massive depopu-
lation would be inevitable. It is, in fact, likely that deficient
floods were ultimately a major check to population growth in
Dynastic Egypt, much as the numbers of gregarious African her-
bivores are naturally maintained somewhat below carrying capacity
by periodic decimation through extreme weather or epidemics.

When deficient floods are the rule on a convex floodplain
over a period of several decades, meander wavelength and amplitude, as well as channel width and depth, readjust. The net effect is that the channel becomes incised, and a new, narrow floodplain at a lower level is created. That such a process has
operated repeatedly in historical times is verified from Aksha
and Meinarti, where the consequences for agricultural settlement
were momentous (de Heinzelin 1964; W. Adams 1965, 1967). Nubia,
however, has a narrow floodplain and responds rapidly with significant vertical change. On the broad alluvial surfaces of Upper Egypt a few centuries would again be required to effect a
proportional change, although specific physical evidence could
only be obtained by detailed study of the suballuvial geology.
Nonetheless, the Bahr Yusef has repeatedly retracted and diver-
ged in response to waning or waxing Nile discharge, and correspondingly desert-margin dunes have either advanced or been under-
cut and removed (see Butzer 1959a, fig. 1). River incision would
have been favored by the declining flood levels of the Old Kingdom at the same time that the greatest part of the fertile silt
would be deposited prior to reaching the downstream sectors of
the Bahr Yusef. In this way nutrient levels were reduced while
the higher salt content of slow-moving, sediment-poor waters

would favor salinization of the outlying basins (see Willcocks
and Craig 1913, pp. 308, 328, 340). In addition, although pre-
cise dating for the geological evidence is lacking, a major period
of dune encroachment in northern Upper Egypt, made possible by restricted flooding and siltation, seems to date to the First Intermediate Period (Butzer 1959b, pp. 110 ff.).

The potential human impact of low Nile floods can be gauged
from Vandier's (1936) and Bell's (1971) reviews of the "lamen-
tations," that is, the pessimistic literature of the period ca.
2250-1950 B.C.[7] Apart from the general implication of inadequate floods, various comments infer a failure of the Nile during
the low-water stage, scarcity of potable drinking water, and extensive desiccation of the Delta marshlands. There are at least
two allusions to forbidding dust storms (increased frequency or
persistence of khamsins?), as well as possible references to
dune activity. The resulting hardships include famines that affected all social classes and at least sizable parts of the valley; general poverty; mass death of adults and children; as well
as reduced birth rates. Mass burials, rotting corpses in the
Nile, suicide, and even cannibalism are also suggested. Anarchy
was commonplace, including mass dislocations of starving people,
risings against the established classes, civil war, conflict and
mass plundering related to roving bands of marauders, as well as
looting of cemeteries, food depots, and private property. Repetitive crop failures were not only a consequence of poor inundations but also of a lack of husbandry, attributed to the prevailing insecurity, but possibly also reflecting on wholesale de-
population.

In a society where the pharaoh was responsible for famine
and plenty, guaranteeing the stability of the cosmic order, one
may indeed wonder how the Egyptians reacted to a succession of

---

7. The three most revealing of these are (1) the tomb inscriptions of Ankhtifi, governor of nomes II and III (see fig. 11)
in southern Egypt, at the beginning of the First Intermediate
Period; (2) the admonitions of Ipuwer, a complex work finalized
at a later date (see Fecht 1972, pp. 10 ff. and postscripts),
but in which the key passages clearly refer to the social upheaval
following the 6th Dynasty; and (3) the prophecy of Neferty, com-
posed during the reign of Amenemhet I, but probably including
allusions to the First Intermediate Period. While there may
well be exaggeration in these descriptions, they equally clearly
serve to illuminate the symptoms of one or more obvious ecological crises.

poor floods and bad harvests (Trigger, forthcoming). Whenever
economic stress, of whatever origin, exceeds the capacity of existing technology and organization, an innovative leadership might
find alternative solutions, whereas an ineffective leadership
would soon be contested and possibly lose its authority. It is
therefore difficult not to see Manetho's allegorical claim of
seventy kings in seventy days at the end of the Old Kingdom[8] as
symbolic of the breakdown of royal authority. Mere mortals of
indifferent ability or questionable motivation could not be expected to exert supernatural control over a river that had failed
to renew the annual lease of life for Egypt.

A reasonable case could be made that the well-entrenched and
probably inflexible bureaucracy of the Old Kingdom did not possess
the requisite ability to cope with impending environmental stress
on a catastrophic scale. Just how well Pepi II (died ca. 2261
B.C.) managed to sustain the national economy during the waning
days of an approximately ninety-year reign is a matter of con-
jecture.[9] In any event, repeated Nile failures brought ecological disaster at a scale sufficient to endanger the existing political, and also possibly the social order (see Bell 1971;
O'Connor 1974) within a few decades or even a few years after his
death.

To what extent the later Ramessids also presided over a
poverty-stricken countryside and a faltering economy is not entirely clear, amid a historical record that emphasizes political
conflicts and foreign invaders. Nonetheless, there are unmistakable economic indicators that Nile floods were primarily mediocre or low during the late Ramessid period: there was a
startling rise in the price of emmer wheat with respect to metals,
beginning during the reign of Ramses III (ca. 1182-1151 B.C.)
and continuing through that of Ramses VII (ca. 1133-1127 B.C.),
rising to eight and even twenty-four times the standard price of
earlier times (Černý 1933, 1954; Janssen 1974b, pp. 550 ff.);

8. See Waddell (1948, p. 57) for the most commonly used version from Africanus. Reference is made to the Seventh Dynasty.

9. Some shifts of administrative policy can be deduced from
the sudden drop in the title ranking of the provincial governors
about midway in Pepi II's reign (see Baer 1960). This may well
represent a reassertion of central authority, possibly related
to major economic crises, to use a modern analogue.

prices then stabilized at a high level until the reign of
Ramses X (1109-1099 B.C.) but fell rapidly before the end of the
dynasty, ca. 1070 B.C. This strongly argues for inadequate harvests ca. 1170-1100 B.C. and implies a generally low Nile, if not
catastrophic failures of the annual flood. Of additional interest is the sharp drop in the price of land at the end of the
21st Dynasty (ca. 945 B.C.), with prices recovering by about
700 B.C., in the 25th Dynasty (Baer 1962). Seen in connection
with the record of unusually high floods at the time, this particular trend may reflect on more extensive inundations, but
political instability and shortage of metal may equally well have
been responsible.

In conclusion, it has become difficult to ignore the possibility that major segments of ancient Egyptian history may be
unintelligible without recourse to an ecological perspective.
Geo-archeological research must be resumed within the Nile floodplain proper, and further refinements are required on the hydro-
logic history of the upper Nile Basin. In this way the times and
amplitudes of environmental change in Dynastic Egypt may one day
be definable to a degree where historical processes can indeed be
reexamined in ecological terms.

6

SPATIAL DISTRIBUTION OF DYNASTIC SETTLEMENTS

Settlement Archeology in Egypt

Human settlements can be studied at two levels: as aggregates, in terms of internal morphology, and as composites, in terms of location and distribution. At each scale, differing aspects of function, interrelationship, and origin provide special foci of potential interest. Such variables are the goal of contemporary settlement geography (see Niemeier 1972, p. 7) and spatial studies (see Haggett 1966). They also are the goal of historical studies, within the constraints imposed by the nature of the archeological or literary record. Trigger (1968), for example, has formulated the objectives of settlement archeology as a matter of location, size, spacing, activities, and material culture of settlements on the one hand, and the interaction of their environmental, economic, and technological determinants on the other.

The last fifty years of Egyptological research have provided a wealth of data in the first, analytical category of Trigger. These data include the patient topographic studies of Gauthier (1925-31), Porter and Moss (1927-51), Otto (1952; see also Nims 1955), Gardiner (1947), Lacau and Chevrier (1956), Montet (1957-61), Kees (1961), Vandier (1961), Sauneron (1964, forthcoming), Fischer (1964), Schlott (1969), and Helck (1974). Equally pertinent are other thematic examinations of settlement morphology (Fairman 1949; Badawy 1954-68; Kemp 1972a, 1972b; O'Connor 1972a; Smith 1972; Kemp and O'Connor 1974; Bietak 1975), land tenure (Gardiner 1948; Hughes 1952; Helck 1958; Baer 1962, 1963; Smith 1972), economic structure (Černý 1954; Helck 1960-64; Kemp 1972b; Janssen 1975), and demography (Baer 1962; O'Connor 1972a, 1972b, 1974; Brothwell and Chiarelli 1973).

There has, however, been little detailed attention to

Trigger's second, essentially functional, category. This is
readily understandable since the data base for adequate study of
macrosettlement patterns in Dynastic Egypt is still being assembled. Furthermore, site studies crucial for an analysis of
microsettlement patterns at the community level are limited to
the ephemeral capital of El-Amarna (Fairman 1949; Kemp 1972b),
the workmen's village of Deir el-Medina (Bruyère 1939, pp. 3 ff.),
the town of Kahun (Petrie 1891), the Ramessid residence Pi-Ramesse (the former Avaris) (Bietak 1975), and the frontier city
of Elephantine (Kaiser et al. 1974). It is regrettable that
earlier generations of archeologists focused their attention on
monumental architecture and cemeteries, rather than habitation
complexes (Redford, forthcoming). In Egypt the result of this
general deficiency in problem orientation is that the most pro-
mising tells have either been destroyed in the search for phosphate
and potash fertilizer (see, for example, Bernand 1971, pp. 132 ff.;
Kemp, forthcoming) or by the rapid settlement expansion of the last
150 years. Those sites that were dug consisted mainly of Saite
to Coptic occupations (ca. 650 B.C.-A.D. 830) that were once remarkably well preserved, but that were ruthlessly stripped away
to get at underlying monuments or in the hunt for papyri (Donadoni, forthcoming; Smith, forthcoming). Sadly lacking as a consequence are critical data on intrasite variability and organic
growth such as have been generated by modern settlement surveys
elsewhere, for example, that of Teotihuacán (see Hammond 1974;
Cowgill 1974).

Although it would be premature to speculate on the demographic structure of Dynastic Egypt or to interpret spatial aspects of sociopolitical activities, there is opportunity for
more synthesis as well as discussion. In particular, it is possible to strive for a more systematic study of settlement distribution in the single ecozone provided by the Nile Valley.
Information of the Faiyum Depression, which represents a distinct ecozone, is provided incidentally during the course of the
discussion. The equally distinctive Delta is not included since
the corpus of information is still too fragmentary for a comparable treatment. However, the available data are summarized
by figure 4, as based on Porter and Moss (1944, pp. 2 ff.),
Gardiner (1948, pp. 132 ff.), Montet (1957), Holz (1969), Bernand (1971), Helck (1974, pp. 151 ff.), and Bietak (1975).

Dynastic Settlements of the Nile Valley

On the basis of the available topographic sources and the
1:100,000 map series, a detailed list of settlements and settlement components has been assembled for the valley from the First
Cataract near Aswan to just south of Cairo (table 2).

A total of 217 Dynastic settlements of reasonable size can
presently be inventoried on the basis of the archeological and
literary records. All of these can be identified with specific
nomes or provinces among the twenty-two Upper Egyptian administrative units, the Faiyum, and the first Lower Egyptian nome.
Some 57% of these sites can be exactly located, with a good degree of certainty, while the great majority of the others can be
situated in their relative sequence, south to north, and with
respect to the western or eastern portions of the floodplain.
As listed in table 2, modern names are transliterated from the
Arabic in accordance with N.A.T.O. policy; ancient designations
are fully capitalized and, wherever possible, are given in their
New Kingdom or Late Dynastic forms, generally following the transliteration scheme of Gardiner (1947).

In view of the inadequate corpus of economic information for
almost all sites, a tally of indirect functional attributes is
given in table 2 under the following heads:

A--Nome capital (underlined and given a score of 3 points)
    or royal residence (shown by X*, with score of 6); if an
    alternative nome capital only, shown by (X) (underlined
    by dashes and given a score of 1);
B--Tombs of the privileged classes or royalty (score of 3
    points), or both (shown by X*, with a score of 4); if the
    necropolis was located away from town, its modern name is
    given after the Egyptian settlement toponym;
C--Mayor ($ḥ₃ty-˓$, see Helck 1974b) (score of 2);
D--Temple, one (score of 2) or more (shown by X*, score of
    3);
E--Settlement (score of 1);
F--Fortress or keep (score of 1);
G--Villa, estate, or suburb attached to site (score of 1);
H--Quarry linked to site (score of 1).

Information on these basic attributes is relatively complete, but
at some unexcavated town sites the tombs of the aristocracy remain to be located, while a few towns with mayors have not been
adequately reported on in the extant literature. The tally of

temple sites is only verifiable in part archeologically; in many
cases the evidence is literary, with mention of the shrine of a
particular god, so that size and significance of temples are unequal; vague allusions to local deities are marked with a query,
but counted positively since the number of temples is almost
certainly underrepresented. Information on whether towns were
walled, or defended by a central fortress, is spotty and could be
augmented by a systematic search of the literary corpus in its
original language.

    This attribute roster does not define the economic functions
of the settlements in question, but it does provide a semiquantitative index of their relative importance as administrative,
religious, or economic centers. Accordingly, an overall cumulative point score is given under the heading I (table 2) and
then interpreted in terms of a fourfold settlement hierarchy:
    1--Large village (score 1-3);
    2--Small center (score 4-6);
    3--Large center (score 7-10);
    4--City (score above 10).
The category "city" includes the two national metropoleis of
Memphis and Luxor-Karnak. Urbanism in the Mesopotamian sense
apparently was uncharacteristic of Egypt (see J.A. Wilson in
Kraeling and Adams 1960, pp. 124 ff.; also Trigger, forthcoming), where the majority of inhabitants of any town were probably engaged in agricultural pursuits. Nonetheless the "centers" and "cities" identified here certainly functioned as market distribution nodes for agricultural products, as locus of
specialized craftsmen or for redistribution of their wares, as
harbors in the almost exclusively riverine communication network, as cult centers closely linked with food storage as well
as administration of the far-flung temple estates, and as a nexus
for the residence and operation of secular landowners and various government officials (see Helck 1958, pp. 211 ff.; Smith
1972; Kemp 1972a; O'Connor 1972a; Kemp and O'Connor 1974). Since
the administrative and particularly the economic functions of
individual towns are poorly known, if at all, and since the
Egyptian terminology for different settlement categories is
vague and probably inconsistent, the functional components and
basic hierarchies proposed in table 2 are relatively objective
and possibly of some value.

    The settlement inventory presented in table 2 is nevertheless

TABLE 2   Documented Dynastic Settlements in the Nile Valley

(Key for letters given at the end of the table)

	A	B	C	D	E	F	G	H	I	J
Nome I (Land of the Bow)										
East Bank										
Aswan (SWEN)				X	X	X		X	5	2
Khattara (?) Kubaniya					X	?		X	3	1
Madinet Ombos (ENBOYET)			X	X*	X	?	X		8	3
Island or West Bank										
Bigga (SENMET)				X	X	X			4	2
Philae (PILAK)				?					2	1
Siheil (SETJET)				X					2	1
Elephantine (YEBU) Kubbet el-Hawa	X	X	X	X*	X	X		X	13	4
Nome II (Throne of Horus)										
East Bank										
Nag el-Kagug (? SUNY)		X			X	X			4	2
? (IAT-GEB)					X				1	1
West Bank										
Gebel el-Silsila (KHENU)		X		X*	?	X		X	9	3
Nag el-Hasaya (?)		X	X	X	?				4	2
Idfu (EDJBO)	X	X	X	X	X	X		X	13	4
? (IAT-NET-RA)					X				1	1
? (IAT-NET-NEG)					X				1	1
Nome III (The Double Plume)										
East Bank										
El-Kab (NEKHAB)	X	X		X*	X				10	3
El-Matana (AGNY)					X				1	1
El-Mialla (PI-HFOET)		X			X				4	2
El-Dibabiya (?)					?			X	2	1
? (HAR-MER)					X				1	1

	A	B	C	D	E	F	G	H	I	J
West Bank										
Kom el-Ahmar (NEKHEN)	(X)	X	X	X	X	X		X	10	3
El-Kola (? PI-ĀNUKI)		X			X				4	2
Kommeir (PI-MERU)				X	X				3	1
? (HO-N-SHEMSU)					X				1	1
Isna (INYET)		X	X	X	X				9	3
? (IA-N-RE-BEKHBEKH)					X				1	1
Asfun (HA-SNOFRU)				?	X		X		4	2
El-Gabalein (PI-HATHOR)		X		X	X	X			7	3
Nome IV (The Plumed Scepter)										
East Bank										
El-Salmiya (?)				?	?				3	1
Tod (DJARTY)				X	X				3	1
? (MEN-IRY)					X				1	1
? El-Bayadiya (IPET REJET)	X*				X				1	1
Luxor-Karnak (WESET)			X	X	X	X	X		14	4
? (UN-SHAY-U)					X				1	1
? (SEKHEM)					X				1	1
El-Madamud (MADU)			X	X	X				3	1
West Bank										
El-Mahamid Qibli (SMEN, IMIOTRU)			X	X	X	?			6	2
El-Rizeiqat (?)				X*	X				1	1
Armant (IWNY)		X	X	X*	X				9	3
El-Qurna (IMENT WESET)		X*			X	X	X	X	11	4
Nome V (The Two Falcons)										
East Bank										
Sheikh Benat Beri (IU-SHEN-SHEN)		X			X	X	X		1	1
Shanhur (P-SHEN-HOR)					X				1	1
Qus (GASY)		X	X	X	X	X	X		7	3
Qift (GEBTYU)	X	X	X	X*	X	X	X	X	13	4

Site	A	B	C	D	E	F	G	H	I	J
? (HESI-E-SE)					X				1	1
West Bank										
? (HRAI-HI-AMUN)					X				1	1
El-Zawayda/Kom Bilal (ENBOET)		X		X	X				6	2
El-Deir/El-Ballas (?)							X		2	1
? (SETF)					X				1	1
Nome VI (The Crocodile)										
East Bank										
? (SHABET)				X	X				1	1
? (BATYU)					X				1	1
? (NEBUTET)					X				1	1
West Bank										
? (UNU)				?	X				3	1
Dandara (INU)	X		?	X*	X		X		13	4
Nome VII (The Bāt Mask)										
East Bank										
El-Qasr wa'l Saiyad (NSHENE-NSET)	X	X	?	?	X			X	7	3
West Bank										
Hiw (HE-SEKHEM)	X	X	X	X	X		X		12	4
? (PI-BOINU)					X		X		2	1
? (HEWARET AMENEMHET)				X	X		X		4	2
? (WAHSUT KHARKHAURE)				?	X		X		3	1
? (PI-MERAB)					X		X		2	1
Abu Tisht (PI-DJODJ)				?	X				3	1
Nome VIII (The Great Land)										
East Bank										
Nag el-Sheikh Mubadir (?)				X	X				1	1
El-Balabish (?)				X	X				1	1
Nag el-Mashayikh (BEHDET IEBTET)		X					X		4	2
West Bank										
? (NIAT)				X	X				1	1
El-Araba el-Madfuna (EBODJU)	X*		X	X*	X	X	X		12	4

Settlement	A	B	C	D	E	F	G	H	I	J
? (N-MAKER-NTENI)					X				1	1
El-Mahasna (?)					X				1	1
Girga (?) Nag el Deir		X	X		X				4	2
El-Birba (TJENI) El-Raqaqna, Beit	X	X*		?	X				12	4
Khallaf										
? (IMU)					X				1	1
El-Manshah (PSOI) El-Hagarsa		X			X				4	2

Nome IX (The Min Symbol)

East Bank

Settlement	A	B	C	D	E	F	G	H	I	J
Akhmim (KHANT-MIN)	X	X	?	X*	X		X	X	14	4
El-Salalumi (?)			?	X	?				3	1
El-Sawama (?)					X				1	1

West Bank

Settlement	A	B	C	D	E	F	G	H	I	J
? (HE-UNAS)							X		1	1
? (NESHYET)				X	X				3	1
Wannina (HET-RIPE)				?	X				3	1
? Sohag (DJA-RUHE)					X				1	1
? (PI-SENGER)					X				1	1
Amba Shinuda (SHAU)				?	X				3	1
Idfu (ITEB)					X				1	1
? (PI-NEKHEB-EN-ISHA)					X				1	1
? (HAK)				?	X				3	1
? (PI-ONKH)				?	X				3	1
? Tahta (HET-TYET) El-Khizindariya					X			X	2	1

Nome X (The Cobra)

East Bank

Settlement	A	B	C	D	E	F	G	H	I	J
Qaw el-Kebir (DJUKA)	X	X			X	X		X	13	4
El-Hammamiya (?)		X			X				4	2
Badari				X	X				1	1
Nag Wisa				X	X				3	1
Sahil Sillim					X				1	1
Mustagidda					X				1	1
El-Khawalid		X		X	X				4	2
El-Matmar					X				3	1

? Include:
PI-MUT-NEB-MEGEB
INMET
PI-WADJOI
MEHEN-NEMTYWEY

	A	B	C	D	E	F	G	H	I	J
West Bank										
Kom Ishqaw (EDJOET)	(X)			?				X	4	2
Kom Isfaht (?)									2	1
Abu Tig (PSHENA) El-Zarabi									1	1
Nome XI (SETH)										
West Bank										
Shutb (SHASHOTEP) Deir Rifa	X	X		X	X	X			10	3
Nome XII (The Viper Mountain)										
East Bank										
Bisra (?)	(X)							X	1	1
? (IAKMET)					1				2	1
? (UNUHA)					1				1	1
? (PI-MUT)					1				1	1
El-Atawla (PI-NEMTY) Deir el-Gabrawi	X	X		X	X		?		10	3
Nome XIII (Upper Nedjfet Tree)										
West Bank										
Durunka (MEDJED)	X	X		X	X				4	2
Asyut (SIYAWTI)		X	X		X				11	4
? (PI-SEKHEMY)					X				1	1
? (NAY-NET-IDEB)					X				1	1
Manqabad (KHAYET)				X	X				3	1
Manfalut (?) Dara, El-Atamna		X*			X				5	2
? (PAGSE)					X				1	1
Nome XIV (Lower Nedjfet Tree)										
East Bank										
Deir el-Quseir (?)		X		X	X				6	2
West Bank										
? (KHAY)				?			X		1	1
El-Qusiya (KOS) Mir	X	X			X				10	3
? (HE-HATHOR)					X				1	1

	A	B	C	D	E	F	G	H	I	J
? (RE-N-HE-NEBETHE)					X				1	1
? (SENENIA)					X				1	1
Nome XV (The Hare)										
East Bank										
Tell el-Amarna (AKHETATEN)		X*	X	X*	X		X	X	[12]	–
Hatnub (HE-NUB)								X	1	1
? (PI-SHES)								X	1	1
Deir el-Barsha (?)									1	1
El-Sheikh Ibada (NAY USIMARE)		X		X*	X				7	3
? (PI-UDJUYU)					X				1	1
West Bank										
Dairut (TJERTI)									1	1
El-Ashmunein (KHMUN, UNU) Sheikh Said	X	X	X	X	X		X		12	4
Tuna (HASROET)				X	X				3	1
? Itlidim (NEFRUSY) Balansura		X		X	X	X			9	3
? (HU-WERE)				X	X				3	1
Hor (H-WOR)				X	X				3	1
Nome XVI (The White Oryx)										
East Bank										
? (ARIT)					X				1	1
? Beni Hasan (MENAT KHUFU)				?	X				3	1
Istabl Antar (PI-NEBONE)				X	X	?			4	2
Kom el-Ahmar (HEBNU) Beni Hasan, Zawyet (R-ONE)	X	X*	X	X	X		X		13	4
Nazlet el-Shurafa				X	X	X			2	1
Tihna (PI-MUI-KHANT)		X			X	?			7	3
West Bank										
? (IROD)				X	X				3	1
? (PI-WADJOI)				X	X				3	1
Nome XVII (The Black Dog)										
East Bank										
Gabal el-Teir (TY-MERWOTEF)		X		X	X				6	2

	A	B	C	D	E	F	G	H	I	J
El-Siririya (PI-HATHOR)	X			X	?			X	4	2
El-Sheikh Fadl (HARDAI)			X	?	X				8	3
West Bank										
? (ANASHA)				X	X				3	1
? (MENONKH)				X	X				3	1
? (IU-NESH)				X	X				3	1
El-Qeis (SAKO)	(X)			X	X	X			5	2
? (HENU)				X	X				3	1

Nome XVIII (The Falcon)

	A	B	C	D	E	F	G	H	I	J
East Bank										
? (U-NEMTY)	X			X*	X				4	2
? (TUHY-EN-ERESET)					X				1	1
Kom el-Ahmar Sawaris (H-NESU)	X	X			X	X	X		11	4
? Sharuna (H-BOINU)				?	X	X			3	1
El-Hiba (TEUDJOI)		X		X	X				7	3

Nome XIX (The Double Scepter)

	A	B	C	D	E	F	G	H	I	J
Bahr Yusef										
El Bahnasa (PI-EMDJE)				X	X				1	1
? (WNSY)				X	X				3	1
? (TJAYEF)			X	X*	X				3	1
El-Qaiyat (SPERMERU)	X			X	X				9	3
? (OPE)				X	X				3	1
? (SHAROPE)				X	X				3	1
? (APA-NUTE)									2	1
? (PI-WAYNA)					X	F			1	1
? (ONAYNA)			X		X				4	2

Nome XX (Upper Naret Tree)

	A	B	C	D	E	F	G	H	I	J
Bahr Yusef and West Bank										
Dishasha (?)					?				4	2
? (JEMY)		X		X	X				3	1
Ihnasya (NINSU)	X	X	X	X*	X		X		13	4

	A	B	C	D	E	F	G	H	I	J
? (ROBANA)									3	1
Near Ghurab (SHE)		X	X	X	X				5	2
Kom Madinet Ghurab (MI-WER)		X	X	X*	X				9	3
El-Lahun (R-EN-HONE)		X		X	X				6	2
El-Haraqa (?)		X			?				3	1
Abu Sir el-Malaq (PI-OSIR)				X	X				3	1
? (SU)				X	X				3	1
? (AMEN-RE)				X	?				3	1
(Settlements of unknown location, listed thematically)										
? (PI-SHAT)				X	X				3	1
? (PI-WADJ)					X				1	1
? (PA-KEN PA-MESHA)					X				1	1
? (IAT PEN-BASTET)					X				1	1
? (IAT-N-WAB)					X				1	1
? (IAT-HEH)					X				1	1
? (IAT-CHAT)					X				1	1
? (IAT-SHA-NENET)					X				1	1
? (NEB SHEF)					X				1	1
? (HU-MONTU)							X		1	1
? (HU-NINSU)							X		1	1
? (HU-NEBES)							X		1	1
? (HU-NEDJES)									1	1
? (SEGER-N-ARU)						X			1	1
? (SEGER-N-HU-TET)						X			1	1
? (BEKHEN-N-PA-NEHESY)						X			1	1
? (BEKHEN-N-NEFER-RENPET)						X			1	1

Faiyum (Land of the Lake)

	A	B	C	D	E	F	G	H	I	J
Hawara (?)	X			X	?		X		7	3
El-Faiyum--Kiman Faris (SHEDYET)		X	X	X	X		X		9	3
Abgig				X	?				3	1
Umm el-Breigat (? TEPDEBN)					X				1	1

	A	B	C	D	E	F	G	H	I	J
Madinet Madi (?)				X	X				1	1
? (DJERT)				?	X				3	1
? (KEM-WER)				?	X				3	1
? (TEP-SEDJEM)					X?				1	1
? (SESHET)				?	X?				3	1
Dimai (?)				X					3	1
Qasr el-Sagha (?)				X	?			X	3	1
Biyahmu (?)				X	X				3	1
? (BEDJDEN)				?	?				3	1
? (RE-SENTY)				?	X				3	1
Seila (?)		X*			X				5	2
? (TEP-TAWY)				?	X				3	1
? (SEHET-WAB)				?	X				3	1
Umm el-Atl (GENU)					X				1	1

Nome XXI (Lower Naret Tree)

West Bank

	A	B	C	D	E	F	G	H	I	J
Maidum (MERTUM)		X*	X	X	X				9	3
El-Riqqa (? SMEN-HOR)					X				1	1
Kafr Ammar (SHENA-KHEN)	X	X			X				7	3
? (PI-SEKRE-NET-SEHED)				X					3	1

Nome XXII (The Flint Knife)

East Bank

	A	B	C	D	E	F	G	H	I	J
Atfih (TPEHU)	X		X	X	X				8	3

Lower Egypt I (The White Palace)

East Bank

	A	B	C	D	E	F	G	H	I	J
El-Masara (?)								X	1	1
Tura (TROAU)		X			?			X	5	2

West Bank

	A	B	C	D	E	F	G	H	I	J
Lisht (ITU-ITAWI)		X		X	?	X			7	3

	A	B	C	D	E	F	G	H	I	J
Dahshur (?)		X*		X	?				7	3
Mazghuna (?)		X		X	?				6	2
? (KHANTUFE)			?	?	X				5	2
Mit Rahina (<u>MENFE</u>) Saqqara	X*	X*	X	X*	X	X	X		18	4
Abu Sir (?)		X*			?	X			8	3
Zawyet el-Aryan (? INBU-HEDJ)		X			?	X			5	2

NOTE: A = Nome capital, B = tombs of nobility or royalty, C = mayor, D = temple, E = settlement, F = fortress, G = villa, estate, suburb, H = quarry, I = cumulative rating, J = overall hierarchical category (see text for details).

incomplete, on two counts. First, with few exceptions, small
villages, hamlets, and dispersed estates or farm complexes--ap-
proximately equivalent to the modern categories *kafr*, *ezbeh*,
and *nag*, respectively--will have had none of the cult and administrative functions to merit mention in the average literary
sources, and their archeological traces are almost never in evidence. With the exception of Papyrus Wilbour, which inventories
the landholdings of a part of northern Upper Egypt (see Janssen
1975b), it is reasonable to assume that other sources refer to
settlements at least equivalent to the administrative village
(*nahieh*) of the nineteenth century (see Boinet 1899). That this
is indeed so can be inferred from Papyrus Wilbour, which lists
416 settlements of all sizes from a total area of only 136 sq
km (see Gardiner 1948; O'Connor 1972a). A second aspect of the
incomplete nature of table 2 is unequal regional representation.
The degree of archeological exploration is variable and, quite
apart from selective destruction of sites by the Nile, practi-
cally none of the occupied town mounds of the Nile Valley have
been investigated and only a minority of abandoned *koms* has ever
been visited. The state of archeological exploration is particularly bad between about El-Birba and the latitude of the Faiyum.
Similar inadequacies can be cited for the literary record, which
is based almost exclusively on New Kingdom records from Luxor
and is increasingly fragmentary for areas north of Dandara. Pre-
servation or discovery is also incomplete, judging by the copious
records of Papyrus Wilbour for parts of nomes XVII-XX.

Theoretically, given a representative number of properly
recorded regions, those settlement components underrepresented in
the remaining regional records might potentially be reconstructed
by use of central place theory. In particular, normal patterns
of central places show an arithmetic progression, with lower-or-
der settlements represented in increasingly larger numbers (see
Haggett 1966). Quite apart from the lowest-order settlement
category, for which we have next to no data, trial plotting of
identified sites for the best-documented nomes showed no inter-
regional consistency whatsoever between bifurcation ratios of
intersettlement distance among settlements of different categories.
Furthermore, the linear arrangement of sites along the floodplain, their preferred location on the banks of the Nile and the
Bahr Yusef (or Bahguriya Canal), and their subtle division

into west- and east-bank spheres, makes central place hexagons in-
appropriate to represent the Nile Valley data.[1] The nature of
the best-fit lattice cannot even be determined with the inadequate number of topographically fixed sites along a river whose
course cannot be reconstructed.

The best that can presently be done for the Nile Valley data
is to apply one of the most basic experiences of central place
studies (Christaller 1966, p. 187), that median bifurcation ratios
of at least 2:1, and ideally 3:1, will be present between successive
settlement hierarchies. This is also the case in Johnson's (1975)
preliminary analysis of the ancient Uruk network. Such a factor
has accordingly been used to provide a rudimentary degree of
standardization to the Egyptian settlement data. The results
are given by table 3, in which the minimum numbers of small centers
and large villages for each nome have been "predicted," using a
bifurcation ratio of 2:1. The small centers are predicted with
respect to the total number of "cities" and "large centers," since
the relatively complete record of "cities" and "large centers" is
sufficiently inconsistent from nome to nome to suggest that
their functional role in regional hierarchical subsystems with
respect to small centers and villages was broadly comparable. If
this assumption--entirely reasonable in a heavily rural society--
were incorrect, the true numbers of small centers would be greater
still.

Overrepresentation is a problem in some nomes, requiring local adjustments (table 3):

1. In nome I, the temples, fortresses, and entrepôt centers
at the Nubian frontier are quite out of proportion with the available agricultural base. The number of small centers has consequently been left unchanged.

---

1. Application of central place theory to archeology has
become increasingly popular and has provided some useful perspectives. However, the mechanics of implementation have not
always been fully comprehended. More importantly, perhaps, the
premises have also been open to question. Central place theory
assumes settlement patterns that reflect primarily on economic
principles such as cost and profit, commodity exchange, and distance decay factors. In a non-monetary economy, with limited
profit orientation (Janssen 1975b), redistribution of agricultural resources can be achieved without a complex hierarchy of
economic centers. In the Egyptian case it is probable that terrain-
related site location, access to riverine transport and irrigation
basins, and the role or status of prominent cult centers played
a primary role in settlement patterning.

2. In nome III, the full weighting of two capitals that were not coeval has fictitiously increased the number of large centers from three to four. The lower number is assumed to be applicable.

3. In nome XX, Papyrus Wilbour provides the unusual problem of literary overrepresentation. Settlements in the category of individual houses and small villages were omitted altogether, in part by following the selection of Montet (1961, pp. 185 ff.). Furthermore, rather than to add yet another small center by theoretical prediction, one large village has here been raised to the status of a small center.

4. For the Faiyum there are a considerable number of unidentified sites that Montet (1961, pp. 211 ff.) has read from the schematic map of the Lake Moeris Papyrus. Table 2 utilizes only those sites confirmed by at least one additional author from other sources. However, there is a probability that several of these were small centers rather than large villages, and the prediction of table 3 has transferred three of the latter to the former category.

5. In nome XXI, the Old Kingdom, Maidum mortuary center provides a fictitious large center that has accordingly been counted as a small center in the prediction of table 3.

6. Finally, Lower Egyptian nome I has a surfeit of mortuary complexes that grossly inflate the number of large centers, two of which have been transferred to the small center category in table 3. These various readjustments do not entirely eliminate overrepresentation, but they do provide a more realistic picture.

A final problem of this settlement inventory is that it spans 2,000 years. The obvious case of the ephemeral royal residence at Amarna was entirely omitted from tables 2 and 3. The Old Kingdom mortuary centers and their satellite settlements in the Memphite region were abandoned after the 6th Dynasty, and nome XXI was probably far less densely settled in later times. Similar objections could be raised for nome XX and the Faiyum, where Middle Kingdom building activities were paramount; here, however, organic growth was maintained at many centers during later periods (see Kemp 1972a). The Theban focus in nome IV first achieved significance after the 6th Dynasty but, after reaching its zenith in the 18th Dynasty, it began to decline with respect to the Delta cities and Memphis during Ramessid times. These generalizations only serve to gloss over the fact that at most sites monumental

Table 3   Dynastic Settlement Patterns in the Nile Valley

Nome (Capital)	Cities	Large Centers	Small Centers	Large Villages	Population Index	Small Centers: Predicted	Large Villages: Predicted	Corrected and Estimated Population (x 1,000)	Area (sq km)	Population Density per sq km x 1,000	Adjusted River Frontage (km)	Ratio of Area to River Frontage
Upper Egypt												
I. (Elephantine)	1	1	2	3	37	2*	4*	39	72	542	42	1.7
II. (Idfu)	1	1	2	3	32	4	8	52	137	380	67	2.0
III. (El-Kab)	..	4	3	6	55	6*	12*	82	225	365	118	1.9
IV. (Karnak)	2	1	1	8	54	6	12	87	284	306	50	5.7
V. (Qift)	1	1	1	6	33	2	6	39	331	118	42	7.9
VI. (Dandara)	1	..	..	4	19	2	4	29	300	97	55	5.5
VII. (Hiw)	1	1	1	4	33	2	4	38	306	124	40	7.7
VIII. (El-Birba)	2	..	3	6	41	4	8	50	613	82	75	8.2
IX. (Akhmim)	1	..	..	13	40	2	13	50	575	87	62	9.3
X. (Qaw)	1	..	3	7	37	3	7	37	531	70	42	12.6
XI. (Shutb)	..	..	..	..	10	2	4	28	125	224	15	8.3
XII. (El-Atawla)	..	1	..	4	15	2	4	25	206	122	30	6.9
XIII. (Asyut)	1	1	2	..	26	2	4	26	250	104	37	6.8
XIV. (El-Qusiya)	..	..	1	4	20	2	4	25	272	92	24	11.3
XV. (El-Ashmunein)	1	1	..	8	42	6	12	80	650	123	52	12.5
XVI. (Kom el-Ahmar)	1	2	1	5	36	2	5	41	377	109	44	8.6
XVII. (El-Sheikh Fadl)	..	1	3	4	35	3	6	39	563	70	43	13.1
XVIII. (Kom el-Ahmar Sawaris)	1	1	1	..	26	2	4	35	425	83	63	6.8
XIX. (El-Qaiyat)	..	1	1	7	25	2	7	30	438	69	35	12.5
XX. (Ihnasya)	1	1	3	23	74	4	22*	80	643	125	54	11.9
FAIYUM (El-Faiyum)	1	2	1	15	58	6	12*	77	400	193	..	..
XXI. (Kafr Ammar)	..	1	..	2	20	2*	4*	34	133	256	19	7.0
XXII. (Atfih)	..	1	..	..	8	2	4	26	200	130	37	5.4

Subtotal	17	24	29	138	776	70	170	1,049	8,056		168.0	
				Lower Egypt								
I. (Memphis)	1	3	4	1	62	4*	8*	76	281	271	46	6.1
Total	18	27	33	139	838	74	178	1,125	8,337			
Average					34.9			47	347.4		172.3	

*Reduced; see text for explanations.

tombs or a fortress were only built over a century or two, while
at other times the same site was no more than a market village.
These complications cannot be eliminated, but fortunately the
bulk of the information utilized here dates to the New Kingdom.
Deletion of the royal mortuary complexes in the north and the
nomarch tombs in the middle reaches of the valley would have provided a picture broadly representative of Ramessid times. This
would shift a number of places from the city to large center categories, without affecting population levels significantly. However, considering that the literary record is particularly incomplete for the same areas, the present compilation is probably preferable.

Demographic Inferences

Bearing in mind the many assumptions and problems basic to
the settlement inventory in table 2, any generalizations or co-
rollary conclusions must be considered with appropriate circum-
spection. Since the implications of the data are great, a higher-
level analysis is warranted, but the reader is forewarned that
none of the numerical data are to be taken literally.

To reiterate, the weighted scores of table 2 are intended to
provide a tally of functional attributes rather than, say, of
monumental architecture. When generalized into the four settlement hierarchies of table 3, organized into nomes, and further
adjusted to eliminate various consistencies of the data, the composite provides a weighted score that is probably roughly *proportional to population level*. The table does not imply that there
were three hundred or even six hundred settlements in the Nile
Valley during the New Kingdom. Rather, it aims to show that the
numbers of intermediate and large-sized settlements varied from
nome to nome, that settlements were clearly concentrated in a few
of these nomes, and that there are semiquantitative criteria for
estimating the degree of agglomeration. The corrected population
index proposed in table 3 means no more and no less. By applying
an arbitrary factor of 1,000, a population figure of 1.1´million
would be obtained for the valley floodplain and Faiyum, which is
within the approximation of 2.4 to 3.6 million for all of Ramessid Egypt suggested by K. Baer (in preparation).

Baer (1962, and in preparation) estimated the density of
rural population on the basis of soil fertility, crop yield (see
Jenny 1962), and caloric intake. He inferred a reasonable carry-

ing capacity of a little less than one person per two arourae,
that is, 184/sq km. In order to compare these data, the best
estimate for the delimitation of the New Kingdom floodplain and
Faiyum was drawn to the base of the 1:500,000 topographic maps,
and an area of 8,337 sq km obtained by planimetry, with a
probable error of ±5%. According to Baer's method, this would imply a rural population of about 1.5 million, a value that could
be increased during times of peak agricultural productivity,
with additional, urban aggregates supported by imports at the
time of imperial expansion. This compares with the first, 1882
census data (considered by G. Baer 1969, pp. 133 ff., to be 15%
too low) of 2.8 million on a cultivable surface of 11,600 sq km
south of Cairo, that is, a density of 240 (alternatively 280)
per square kilometer, at a time when irrigation technology was
far more sophisticated and improving rapidly. In other words, the
nome population suggested in table 3 may provide crude *approxi-
mations* of real population numbers for the New Kingdom.[2]

Turning to the areas of the individual nomes, it is readily
apparent that the nome boundaries given by Montet (1961, folding
map) and Helck (1974) are not in complete agreement. Montet
(1961, pp. 9 f.) adopts a series of measures attached to each
nome by the chapel inscriptions of Sesostris I at Karnak (see
Lacau and Chevrier 1956) as units of area and ostensibly uses
these to help define his nomes. Planimetry of Montet's mapped
nomes showed no resemblance to these figures. Schlott (1973),
Graefe (1973), and Helck (1974, pp. 13 f.) have more convincingly

2.   Fekri Hassan has kindly allowed me to see and quote an
unpublished manuscript of his, entitled "Pyramid Building: An
Anthropological Perspective." His estimates of Dynastic population size are based on an interesting line of reasoning: allowing for 16% of the total cultivable land for buildings, vegetables, orchards, and flax, and a yield of 1,650 lb of wheat
per acre and 1,560 lb barley per acre (figures based on Papyrus
Wilbour and modern analogues), a total of 2.7 billion lb of
grain would have been produced annually on 8,000 sq km. Sub-
tracting 45% for seed stock, trade, and taxes, about 1.5 billion
lb would be available for home consumption. With an estimated
food intake of 1.06-1.27 lb per person per day (a figure comparing well with that for Latin America), the maximum population
that could be supported would be about 3.5 million persons.
However, given the fluctuations of flood level, epidemics, and
so on, actual population size was more likely to be 60% of carrying capacity, that is, close to two million for the Nile floodplain and Faiyum. This approximation compares so closely with
population density in A.D. 1882 that it cautions against assuming
an *average* valley density in excess of 280 sq km until the end of
the last century.

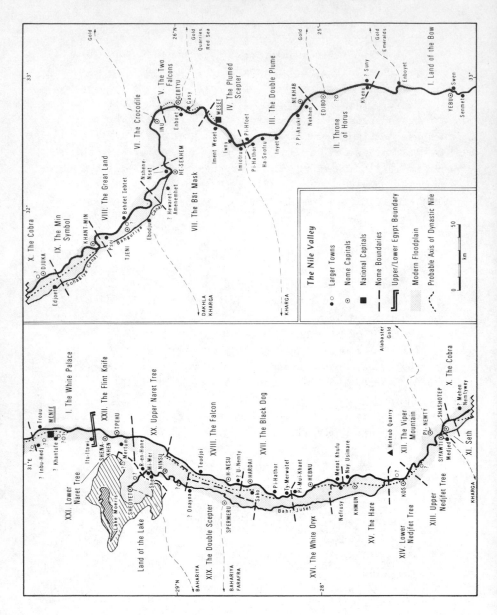

Fig. 11.--Settlement distribution in the Nile valley during Dynastic times. Villages are not shown.

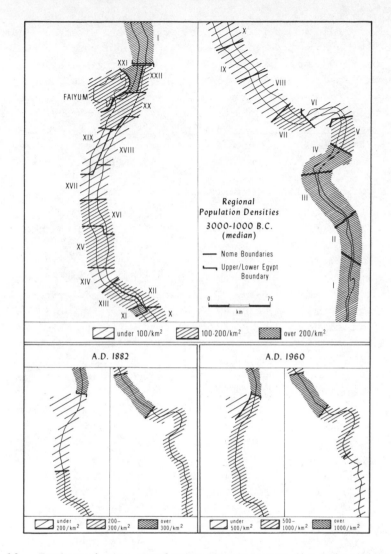

Fig. 12.--Estimated nome population densities in the Nile valley during Dynastic times (see table 2). Comparative densities are also shown for the same provinces (*mudiriyets*) in A.D. 1882 and 1960.

argued that they can be utilized as units of length--in the Nile Valley but not in the Delta (see Bietak 1975, pp. 160 ff. and fig. 33)--and Helck successfully applied them to estimating nome

length along the river. However, minor disagreements can be
voiced as to Helck's borders in the sixteenth to nineteenth nomes,
where river shifts have complicated the issue of west- and east-
bank nomes or nome boundaries. Without detailing the arguments,
the boundaries drawn for this sector in figure 11 are probably in
closer agreement with the supposed topography, the allegiances
of particular towns to the deities of the eighteenth and nineteenth
nomes (see Montet 1961, pp. 176 ff., 181 ff.), and the attri-
bution of Tihna to the sixteenth nome on the basis of its traditional funerary links (see Montet 1961, p. 161). The areas attributed to the nomes (as shown on fig. 11) are given by table 3.
It requires no emphasis that they bear no resemblance to the nome
areas inferred by Montet (1961, pp. 9 ff.).

Applying these figures to the population estimates, nome
densities varied from under 75/sq km (nomes X, XVII, and XIX) to
500/sq km or more (nome I). A median nome density of 172/sq km
compares with a Nile Valley mean of 135/sq km, reflecting greater
densities in a number of relatively small nomes. Figure 12 shows
the distribution of nomes with sparse, intermediate, or dense
settlement, and compares the regional contrasts with those of 1882
and 1960 censuses (see also the contemporary land use data of
Wilson 1955). Regardless of the flaws of the data base, it is
clear that in New Kingdom times the Egyptian population was most
dense between Aswan and Qift and again in the Faiyum and Memphite
regions. It is noteworthy that large segments of the intervening
floodplain were very thinly settled, particularly the areas between
modern Girga and Qaw, and between Minya and El-Fashn. In the nineteenth century A.D., Girga province as well as the region of Cairo
provided the major concentrations of settlement, emphasizing
that the most developed nomes of New Kingdom Upper Egypt did not
coincide with those of today. Furthermore, the Nile Valley was
by no means uniformly settled, and population levels do not appear
to have been uniformly geared to a single carrying capacity. Instead, figure 12 shows that centers of population were evidently
disparate and locally aggregated, in perplexing patterns that
pose a host of historical, economic, and environmental problems.

7

DEMOGRAPHIC DEVELOPMENT AND LAND USE

The available Egyptian evidence, combined with a selection
of external paleodemographic and cross-cultural ethnographic
materials, allows little more than speculation as to the evolution of demographic patterns through time.

The tragedy of Egyptian archeology is that it once provided
a wealth of cemeteries with large skeletal populations. Until
quite recently, however, this material was effectively destroyed
rather than scientifically studied. Skulls were removed from context for trivial "racial" measurements (see, for example, Derry
1956), and the disarrayed postcranial materials were left to
deteriorate. With rare but notable exceptions, primarily resulting from the Nubian salvage programs of the 1960s (see, for
example, Anderson 1968; Greene and Armelagos 1972; Greene 1972;
J. Jungwirth and E. Strouhal, in preparation), there was no
full demographic sampling; in fact, there is a lack of even rudimentary data on such essential items as male versus female
longevity, male stature, or fecundity as estimated from the approximate number of births per female pelvis. Proper study
could have provided critical information on diet, social conditions, and endemic or epidemic disease (see Brothwell and
Chiarelli 1973). O'Connor (1972b, 1974) provides examples of
the qualified value of archeological sampling in some of the
better-excavated cemeteries, but the basic paleodemographic
problem remains, for the present, unsolvable.

The only alternative open at present is to attempt a work-
ing hypothesis of demographic trends in ancient Egypt by analogy
and intuitive appraisal of the evidence. Such a patently speculative approach has its merits, by allowing specific problem
formulation. But *caveat emptor*! The numerical values so generated

cannot be cited as real figures. The approximate area of cultivable
land at various times can be crudely estimated, by giving due attention to the physical history discussed above (see also Butzer
1961, 1974), and by assuming that the maximum productivity of the
Greco-Roman period coincided with a cultivated area approximately
equal to that of 1882. The second variable is population density,
which can be estimated from agricultural yield (Baer 1962), from
the settlement inventory presented above, and by analogy. From
these hypothetical values an even more questionable population
norm can be suggested for successive periods of optimal ecological prerequisites and social stability. Finally, negative deviations from this trajectory can be inferred from the body of
historical and physical evidence. The results of this exercise are
given by table 4 and figure 13, and a discussion of the argumentation and implications follows, organized regionally.

The Nile Valley

The area of cultivable floodplain at times of reasonably good
floods has remained basically similar, except from the perspective
of technology. The rudimentary flood-irrigation farming practiced
from Predynastic through Middle Kingdom times had access to comparable areas on the order of 8,000 sq km. The appearance of the
shaduf in Upper Egypt during the 18th Dynasty suggests that mechanical lift irrigation would now allow some summer cropping on the
levees, and an expansion of agriculture along the valley margins.
A 10% to 15% increase in arable land is therefore posited by
Ramessid times, with another, similar increase following the introduction of the saqiya early in the Ptolemaic period.

Early Bronze Age settlement estimates from Greece provide
potential clues for the Badarian occupation of the Nile floodplain ca. 4000 B.C. In the Greek example, Renfrew (1972) suggests regional population densities of 2.5 to 14 persons per
square kilometer, while Angel (1972) provides grounds for a general estimate of 10/sq km based on the premise that 65% to 80% of
the surface was not cultivable. This value is consonant with
ethnographic analogues for simple agricultural communities (see
Braidwood and Reed 1957; Sanders and Price 1968, pp. 78 ff.).
Assuming that 75% (instead of 25%) of the accessible Nile floodplain was actually utilized, this would imply a density of 30/sq
km and a total population in the order of 0.25 million.

Optimal prehistoric settlement density in Greece was achieved

Table 4 Hypothetical Demographic Development in Ancient Egypt

Region	4000 B.C.			3000 B.C.			2500 B.C.			1800 B.C.			1250 B.C.			150 B.C.		
	A	B	C	A	B	C	A	B	C	A	B	C	A	B	C	A	B	C
Valley	8,000	(30)	240	8,0C0	(75)	600	8,000	(130)	1,040	8,000	(140)	1,120	9,000	(180)	1,620	10,000	(240)	2,400
Faiyum	100	(30)	3	1C0	(60)	6	100	(90)	9	450	(135)	61	400	(180)	72	1,300	(240)	312
Delta	8,000	(10)	80	7,0C0	(30)	210	9,000	(60)	540	10,000	(75)	750	13,000	(90)	1,170	16,000	(135)	2,160
Desert			25			50			25			25			25			50
Total (millions)	0.35			0.87			1.6			2.0			2.9			4.9		

NOTE: A = area of cultivable land in square kilometers, B = population density per square kilometer, C = hypothetical population in thousands.

by the Late Bronze Age, with Renfrew (1972) giving figures of
4.5/sq km to 63.5/sq km, Lukermann (1972) assuming comparability
with conditions in A.D. 1800--implying a density of 25/sq km to
35/sq km, and Angel (1972) arguing for a general value of 30/sq
km. Converting this once again by a factor of three, we obtain
a Nile floodplain density of 90/sq km that must be increased by
at least 50% to take into account the increased productivity as-
sured by artificial irrigation in Old and Middle Kingdom times.
This implies a population of roughly 1.1 million for the more
prosperous millennia of the Old and Middle Kingdoms. Intermediate values are inferred for the 1st Dynasty, ca. 3000 B.C.,
and declines of at least one-third are suggested for the First
Intermediate Period, ca. 2100 B.C., and the Hyksos era, ca. 1600
B.C.

The New Kingdom and Hellenistic periods saw not only a modest
expansion of the cultivated land, but guaranteed increasingly
higher levels of minimum carrying capacity by assuring at least
lift-irrigation agriculture during times of low floods. Table 4
and figure 13 accordingly suggest increasing densities, and a
population expanding to 1.6 million in Ramessid times and perhaps
2.4 million under the early Ptolemies. Although the densities
suggested by tables 3 and 4 are not identical, they are reasonably
close, within the ±15% range of error that must be assumed for both
approaches. The figures derived in table 3 probably tend to the
high side, whereas the estimates of table 4 are more conservative.
The discrepancies should serve to remind the reader that both
methods of reconstruction are fraught with assumptions and uncer-
tainties.

Assuming that the figures provide crude estimates that nonetheless are proportional to the actual demographic development,
discussion is called for.

Pressure on the land must have been low in Predynastic times.
This suggests that land use would have been relatively extensive,
with a substantial component of pastoralism (see Boessneck 1953;
Zeuner 1963; Epstein 1971), and would have allowed for a continued
dependence on a wide array of "gathered" food resources, such as
wild grasses and other vegetable plants (see Clark 1971), fish and
wildfowl (see Gaillard 1923; Brunton and Caton-Thompson 1928;
Edel 1961-64; Helck 1960-64, pp. 816 ff.; Churcher 1972, pp. 124
f.), as well as large mammals (see Butzer 1959a, pp. 78 ff.; Edel

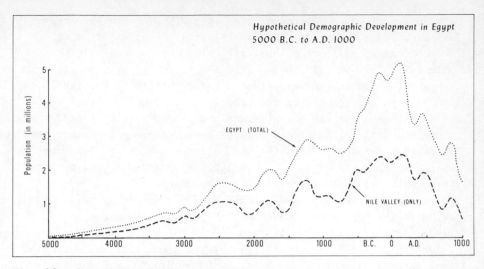

Fig. 13.--Hypothetical demographic development in Egypt 5000 B.C.-
A.D. 1000 (see table 3).

1961-64; Churcher 1972, pp. 125 ff.; Hassan 1975, chap. 5).[1]
Only a small part of the flood basins was planted with emmer wheat,
barley, vegetables, and flax, with degraded riverine woodland vy-
ing with expanding date palm groves[2] along the levees of the Nile
and its seasonal branches such as the Bahr Yusef.

     Predynastic settlement sites were located on the same levees,
free from all but unusually high floods, as well as on the desert
edge. Perhaps half of the floodplain consisted of disturbed savanna and thickets, extensively used for food collecting and seasonal herding of cattle, short-haired goats, hairsheep, and donkeys.

     1. The osteological data on animal bone from habitation
sites are highly unsatisfactory, being primarily identified by non-
specialists, and numerical data are lacking. Nonetheless, the
distinct impression obtains that wild animal bones are abundant at
Predynastic sites.

     2. The long-fronded tree commonly shown on decorated Nagada
II ware may well represent palms. Larsen (1957) has argued for
an identification with the so-called false banana, *Musa ensete*,
of highland Ethiopia. This is by itself implausible on ecological
grounds, since *Musa* has a very circumscribed range in the moister
part of the tropical montane zone. The representations in
question have an "eye" at the core of their canopy that is identical to that in most 18th-Dynasty palm representations; they lack
only fruits to clinch the argument for date or dum palms. It is
pertinent that dates constituted an essential part of the Egyptian
diet (Janssen 1975b).

During the flood season these herds were withdrawn to the levees
or desert edge, where grazing was relatively scarce in the domain of household pigs and poultry. Fish were abundant in the
Nile at all seasons (including Nile perch, catfish, *Synodontis*,
Mormyrus, *Tetradon*, and spawning mullets), with soft-shelled turtle
and hippopotamus providing additional aquatic foods. Great swarms
of migratory ducks, geese, pigeons, and ibis were also resident
among the many waterways and marshes during the winter half-year.
Rhinoceros, elephant, giraffe, and hartebeest were still common
in parts of the floodplain, where lion, leopard, and cheetah com-
peted with the hunter. Forays into the desert in search of oryx,
addax, Barbary sheep, ibex, gazelle, and ostrich are also implied by the representational art. Predynastic subsistence was
clearly diversified in a rich and varied natural environment, in
which irrigation farming initially played a relatively minor role.
Land-use analogues from the Senegal and middle Niger floodplains
of the early nineteenth century are probably appropriate.

Population would appear to have quadrupled in the 1,500-year
period preceding the apex of the Old Kingdom, suggesting a net
growth rate of modest proportions (0.8 per 1,000) but placing
considerable pressure on resources. This may be inferred from
several indirect symptoms that can be read from the drastic change
of land use patterns. First of all there is the evidence of the
literary record, that grain crops now formed the staple food (see
Baer 1962, 1963), supported by an increasing measure of artificial irrigation (see above), which in return required considerable
concentrations of labor in times of excessive flood, to regulate
water intake or drainage without masonry gates, or to build major
transverse or longitudinal dikes. Furthermore, extensive pastoral use of the floodplain was declining, with the Hekanakht
letters (see Baer 1963) suggesting equal proportions of pasture
and crops by 2000 B.C. Second, the almost total disappearance
of large game from the valley, with increasing importation of
captured animals for symbolic hunts by the nobility (Butzer 1959a,
pp. 96 ff.),[3] argues for eradication of most of the natural

3.   Clark (1971) incorrectly interprets the enclosures shown
on the Beni Hasan frescoes as hunting nets. That such nets are
fenced enclosures, used only since the 6th Dynasty (Mereruka),
can be seen from their schematic representation as frames for

vegetation. Only the fish and migratory fowl (see Edel 1961-
1964) remained as a predictable natural resource, with fish a
basic staple for the typical Egyptian meal (Helck 1960-64,
pp. 816 ff.; Janssen 1975b; also Gamer-Wallert 1970), although
legal access to wildfowl may now have been reserved for the pri-
veleged. Third, the first monumental architecture of the Early
Dynastic period at Hierakonpolis (Fairservis 1972), Abydos, and
in the Memphite region (Edwards 1971) already appears symptomatic
of a multitiered economy, and the great building efforts of the
Old Kingdom pharaohs in the last area would have required immense
resources of labor. Apparent barracks to hold at least 4,000
workmen have been found near the Chephren pyramid (Edwards 1961,
pp. 216 ff.), and the seasonal employment of as many as 100,000
able-bodied men[4] presupposes a considerable population base.
Using a Mesoamerican analogy from Sanders and Price (1968, pp.
78 ff.), such activities could hardly be sustained with a density of less than 100 persons per square kilometer.

Presumably the terminal Nagada period witnessed the critical
stages of the shift from pastoralism to crop cultivation, to an
almost total dependence on produced rather than gathered foods,

---

pictures of the hunt, in part set up within the floodplain (show-
ing large trees and water birds), in part on the low desert
(hummocky, sandy surfaces with desert shrubs). The mixture of
habitat-specific animals, such as gazelles (desert), and geese
and wild cattle (floodplain, see Churcher 1972, p. 126) together
in the desert, or of ducks, flamingos, oryx, and gazelle together
on the floodplain, leaves no doubt that the animals were collec-
ted into game parks from diverse ecozones. The sensitivity of
at least the Old Kingdom artists to the life cycle and habitat
of animals is convincingly shown by Edel's (1961-64) meticulous
evaluation of the reliefs and texts in the 5th-Dynasty Chamber of
the Seasons of Neussere.

4. Hassan ("Pyramid Buidling: An Anthropological Perspective," unpublished) finds the traditional figure of Herodotus
(II:126) reasonable, by estimating a labor force of 84,000 em-
ployed eighty days a year for twenty years to erect the Great
Pyramid. Whatever the best figures, such a massive conscription
of labor poses organizational questions. The population of the
Memphite nome was far too small to provide more than a fraction
of this work force. The remainder may have been drawn exclusively
from Lower Egypt, which in the Old Kingdom appears to have been
administered by the king and his closest retainers rather more
directly than was Upper Egypt.

increasingly successful adaptation to natural basin irrigation,
and a greater and greater reliance on artificial irrigation.

National projects such as pyramid building suggest that the
Old or Middle kingdoms saw development of some form of govern-
ment-controlled program to collect, store, and, in times of need,
redistribute food. Direct evidence is lacking, except for per-
functory claims by the pharaoh or his nomarchs to have fed the
hungry in times of need. Furthermore, the known, Old Kingdom
storage facilities were part of mortuary temple complexes, while
the long rows of beehive granaries verified from the Middle Kingdom (both architecturally and in the form of models, Badawy
1966, pp. 31 ff.) were all privately owned. However, the "Gra-
nary of Amun" at Thebes, under Amenhotep II and III (1453-1419
and 1386-1349 B.C., respectively), was of impressive dimensions
(Davies 1929). At least forty pyramid bins, which at Amarna had
an average capacity of 28 cu m (Whittemore 1926), are schematical-
ly shown in Tomb 48 (see Davies 1929, fig. 10). The interplay of
secular and religious functions is also significant, with the
pharaoh viewed as the priest of the harvest and Sen-nufer, the mayor
of Thebes under Amenhotep II, serving as overseer of the granaries
of Egypt (Davies 1929). At their most efficient, the temples of the
New Kingdom functioned as an adjunct of the government (Kemp
1972a; Janssen 1975b) and probably contributed in a significant
way to the managerial skills that regulated the basic food supply
(Kemp 1972a; see also Helck 1958, pp. 152 ff. on distribution).[5]
They may thus have served to mediate between the fat and the lean
years. By mitigating local food shortages in bad years and serving to protect adequate seed stock, at least the New Kingdom tem-

5. The most striking evidence to this effect is that of the
temple plans themselves. The great magazine blocks, not only at
Thebes but, for example, in the temple of Seti I (1291-1279 B.C.)
at Abydos, or at Sesabi and Aksha in Nubia, represent storage ca-
pacities far in excess of even wealthy private individuals, as
visible at Amarna. They imply a significant governmental inter-
vention in the country's economy that presumably would have had
a regulating effect--even though it may not have been intended
in quite that way (Barry J. Kemp, personal communication). The
literary evidence of corruption and inefficiency among the temple staff during the late 20th Dynasty suggests that the system
was breaking down in the troubled times of that period.

ples were potentially able to avert catastrophic famines. Such
institutions could function effectively only as long as government-
guaranteed public order and discipline were maintained in their
internal administration. Deficient Nile floods would therefore
have had disproportionately serious effects during times of
feeble government or unbridled corruption, presumably favoring
population loss following the breakdown of the Old, Middle, and
New Kingdoms.

Irrigation technology appears to have been repeatedly improved during the Pharaonic period, the shift from natural to
artificial flood irrigation accomplished by late Predynastic
times, the shift to lift irrigation well under way during the 18th
Dynasty and effective by Roman times. No such innovations are
apparent among the other agricultural methods. As Erman (1885,
p. 569) pointed out, the ancient Egyptian plowed with a long
wooden aard, drawn by a team of oxen that was led by a second man.
No significant changes of plow type are apparent through time, and
identical wooden hoes continued to be used for harrowing (Erman
1885, pp. 570 f.). The numerous pictorial representations all
agree that seeds were broadcast on unprepared soil, rather than
planted in plow furrows or hoe-turned beds. The limited use of
plow and even hoe preparation in Islamic times (Niemeyer 1936,
table 2) suggests that manual preparation was restricted to
drier locales or horticultural plots. Nile topsoil regularly
flooded by silt-laden "red" water is of high natural fertility.
But nitrogen content decreases by two-thirds in the topmost
50 cm (Jenny 1962), so that the zone of maximum fertility is
shallow, militating against deep plowing. Nitrogen is volatilized
from higher ground by relatively rapid decomposition. Consequently
the levees and lands on the floodplain periphery would require
both preparation and fertilizer.

Until the nineteenth century, when repeated cropping led to
a search for sebakh and the importation of natural or chemical
fertilizers, bird droppings and night soil were exclusively utilized, since other forms of manure were required as fuel in modern
(Niemeyer 1936, p. 67) as well as ancient times (Černý 1955;
Schnebel 1925, pp. 87 ff.). Perhaps, therefore, the traditional
dovecotes already provided fertilizer for high-lying fields and
summer crops in Dynastic Egypt. Yet a single planting season
within the flood basins proper is insufficient to deplete the soil,
particularly if grains and legumes are alternated from year to

year. Consequently fertilizers can have been of little concern
until the beginnings of New Kingdom lift irrigation. This may
explain the limited explicit references to nitrogen-binding fodder crops, such as bersim and fenugreek, until Ptolemaic times
(see Helck 1960-64, pp. 802, 807, as compared with Schnebel 1925,
pp. 87 ff. or Crawford 1971, pp. 112 ff.). Although fodder crops
must have been essential as pasture and dry feed for livestock when
cropland began to displace natural pasturage, the texts are
uniformly parsimonious in their reference to such crops. The
Hekanakht letters (James 1962, p. 59) and Papyrus Wilbour (Gardiner 1948, pp. 22 ff., 60 f.) allude to produce, food, or her-
bage for cattle, and there are relatively frequent references to
plots used for grazing horses, cattle, or goats in the latter.
Yet it remains unclear whether unimproved pasture or fodder crops
are referred to, and grain may have been fed to cattle and goats
(Janssen 1975b), although bersim has been identified from a 12th-
Dynasty burial at Kahun (Loret 1892, p. 95). In any event, it
appears that the potential of such nitrogen-binding crops as ferti-
lizing agents was either immaterial, ignored, or not understood.

Fallow, a vital practice to restore irrigated Mesopotamian
soils and to lower their saline water table (Gibson 1974) was next
to unnecessary in Dynastic Egypt[6] except in areas of lift irrigation. Even in Ptolemaic times it was far from a general practice (see Schnebel 1925, pp. 87 ff.). A major reason is that
salinization was no real problem in the Nile Valley prior to the
introduction of perennial irrigation a century or so ago. Specifically, the summer water table is at least 3-4 m below the surface
in most areas, with 4 to 6 weeks of subsequent inundation assuring
that no salts could build up within the root zone. The one danger
was slow-moving "white water," from which the silt has been deposited in basins or trapped by canals upstream, leaving only
clays and an increasing concentration of sodium-rich solubles.
Those peripheral floodplain areas reached by limited amounts of
white water were therefore subject to salinization, particularly
during intervals of decreasing Nile discharge.

It is apparent that the conservatism of nonirrigation agricultural techniques in Dynastic Egypt was reasonable in view of

6. A suggestive case of fallow in late Ramessid times is
provided in a letter translated by Černý (1939, p. 11), which
refers to three, once-cultivated plots that are to be cleared
of brush.

the amazing fertility of the basin lands with a single cropping
season. This conservatism also applies to the inventory of cultigens. No new cereal or vegetable crops can be verified until
Ptolemaic or even Roman times (see Dixon 1969). Livestock breeding was another matter. Experimental domestication with hyena,
addax, oryx, gazelle, and ibex in Old Kingdom times (see Boessneck 1953; Zeuner 1963, pp. 421 f., 434 f.) suggests a flair
for innovation. Furthermore, the more versatile Asiatic wool
sheep was introduced early in the Middle Kingdom, and soon dis-
placed the traditional fleeceless, hairsheep (Keimer 1938; Zeuner
1963, pp. 180, 183 ff.). The Hyksos introduced the horse (Joachim Boessneck, in preparation), and the first evidence of zebu
strains among Egyptian cattle dates to the 18th Dynasty (Montet
1954; Zeuner 1963, p. 226; Epstein 1971). The camel only came
into general use as a beast of burden in Ptolemaic times (Zeuner
1963, pp. 350 ff.).

A third era of declining productivity and population loss between the later Ramessid reigns and the devastating Assyrian in-
vasions of 667 and 664 B.C. appears to be supported by the im-
poverished cemetery record of Egypt,[7] the total abandonment of
Lower Nubia (Trigger 1965, pp. 112 ff.; W. Adams 1967; Säve-
Söderbergh, forthcoming), and the practical implications of substantially reduced Nile volume (fig. 5). The population of Lower
Nubia began to decline during the second half of the 18th Dynasty
and the region was abandoned not long after the reign of Ramses II.
Although socio-economic processes are also indicated, it is very
probable that agriculture became next to impossible without large-
scale application of lift irrigation, once the Nile began to down-
cut its bed and failed to flood the alluvial lands on a regular
basis.

Lift irrigation was revolutionized by the introduction of
the saqiya during the early Ptolemaic hegemony. Coupled with a
taut and well-conceived entrepreneurial system, Egyptian agriculture under the Ptolemies was expanded and intensified to a
degree unmatched until a century ago, after the introduction of
perennial irrigation. Maximum development and population level
appear to have been reached early in the first century A.D., in

7. Barry J. Kemp: personal communication.

response to an exploitative, labor-intensive agriculture designed
to supply Rome with food (Johnson and West 1949, pp. 132 f.).
It is worth emphasizing that peak population coincided not with
maximum prosperity but with the period of optimal colonial development and exploitation (compare the thesis of Polgar 1972).
However, the 7.5-million population estimate of Josephus for all
Egypt exceeds that of the census of A.D. 1882 and must be considered unacceptable. More reasonable is Russell's (1966) alternative figure of 4.5 million, based on the Idfu temple record
for nine million arourae (24,600 sq km, comparing well with
27,659 sq km in A.D. 188?) (Schlott 1969) under cultivation in the
second century B.C. The alternative figure of 3 million from
Diodorus (I.31:8) in the (?) unemended text is patently too low.[8]
As a compromise, a population of just under 5 million is proposed
in table 4.

   In later Roman, Byzantine, and early Islamic times the population level once again declined rapidly as a result of managerial incompetence, religious strife and civil war, epidemics, and
the devastations of Arabian beduin (see Butzer 1960a; Russell
1966). The details for that period are equally controversial (see
Prominska 1972, for a lack of cemetery evicence for mass deaths
or population dynamics) but are beyond the scope of this study.

The Faiyum Depression

   The Faiyum or "Land of the Lake" retained a unique administrative status throughout the Dynastic era (see Helck 1974, pp.
124 f.). Yet Nagada II settlement extended into the depression,
and Lake Moeris was an integral part of the Egyptian religious
universe since time immemorial (Kees 1961, pp. 196, 224 f.). Old
Kingdom quarries, temples, quays, and restricted lakeshore settlements appear to be verified (Caton-Thompson and Gardner 1929,
1934; Shafei 1940; Said, Albritton, et al. 1972), but most of
the basin was still submerged, so that an arable surface of 100
sq km and a low population density are estimated in table 4. Development was only begun in the 12th Dynasty (see above), when
cultivation expanded to a maximum of 450 sq km. By New Kingdom

---

8. If the 3 million rather than the 7 million version is
accepted, it is still necessary to explain the implication that
Egypt's population had previously been 7 million: Diodorus
visited Egypt at a time when the population had been expanding
for several centuries.

times, settlement density was certainly greater than that of the
Nile Valley (see also tables 2 and 3), although there is next to
no archeological confirmation. Then, during the third century B.C.
the Ptolemies expanded cultivation to about 1,300 sq km, developing
the depression very intensively. At the time of maximum prosperity population was probably in excess of 300,000, with a minimum of 198 settlements still recorded in Byzantine times (Wessely
1904), compared with only 100 in A.D. 1315 (Salmon 1901) and 69
in A.D. 1800 (see Jacotin 1826, sheets 18-19).

The persistence of a large, freshwater lake with extensive
seasonal swamp tracts in the Faiyum raises the possibility that
malaria may have been a major problem. There is no information
from the Faiyum directly, and the whole issue of malaria in
historical Egypt is puzzlingly inconclusive. Textual descriptions
of disease symptoms, such as Papyrus Ebers, include no convincing
example of malaria, and two cases of enlarged spleens on Coptic
mummies can equally well be attributed to bilharzia (see Halawani
and Shawarby 1957; Kamal 1967, pp. 284 f.; Ghalioungui 1969; Zulueta 1973). In fact, the low incidence of sickle-cell anemia
among modern Egyptians suggests that the Mediterranean malaria
parasite *Plasmodium falciparum* has not been endemic in the past.[9]
Nonetheless, examinations of mummy pathology have traditionally been
routine, lacking attention to the crucial evicence of porotic
hyperostosis in bone tissue (see Angel 1972).

The Delta

As elaborated earlier, the major part of the Predynastic
Delta was by no means a marshy wasteland, inhabited only by scattered pastoral communities. Such a conclusion is compatible with
the antiquity of the Delta's cult centers and the fact that the
Delta was *the* Lower Egypt of the semimythical wars of unification in the late fourth millennium B.C. (Kaiser 1964). In fact,
the ten oldest of the twenty Lower Egyptian nomes predate the

9. The endemic mosquito of modern Egypt is *Anopheles pha-*
roensis, very abundant in the Delta, but little interested in
man (Juan de Zulueta, personal communication). The malaria epidemic of 1942-43 was a result of penetration of the very effective, anthropophytic *Anopheles gambiae* from the upper Nile to
as much as 25 km north of Asyut (Shousha 1948). It appears
probable that *A. gambiae* was never a serious threat in the cooler
environment of the Delta.

3rd Dynasty (Helck 1974, pp. 199 f.) and are significantly situated between the Delta distributaries (Kaiser 1964). Furthermore, over thirty towns north of Cairo are verified archeologically or epigraphically by the end of the Middle Kingdom (fig. 4).

It is nonetheless probable that settlements were far more
dispersed than they were in Upper Egypt, that overall population
density was significantly lower, and that the northernmost one-third
of the Delta was almost unpopulated in Old Kingdom times. In effect, a considerable body of information can be marshalled to
show that the Delta was underdeveloped and that internal colonization continued for some three millennia, until the late Ptolemaic
era.

The continuing availability of prime land is suggested by the
example of Metjen, a 3rd- to 4th-Dynasty overseer of royal estates
(vineyards, orchards, flax) in nomes II and IV-VI, who "founded"
twelve villages (see Sethe 1933, § 3; Kees 1961, p. 185; Baer
1963). Similarly, 338 Lower Egyptian versus 168 Upper Egyptian
domains show a decided preference for the Delta as a locus for new
estates, with the largest 5th-Dynasty temple donations being made
in Lower Egypt (Jacquet-Gordon 1962; Sethe 1933, § 240-49). The
pharaoh Merikare (10th Dynasty, ca. 2070 B.C.) was advised to
"build cities in the Delta," and a Ka-house of Akhtoy, the father
of Merikare, is indeed recorded on a later, 12th-Dynasty stele at
Pi-Ramesse (Bietak 1975, p. 102). Altogether, Kees (1961, pp.
185 ff.) has argued for continuing reclamation and winning of new
cultivable land by irrigation and drainage.

At the same time, pastoralism was and remained a major economic
pursuit, as can be deduced from several lines of indirect evidence:

1.   Ancient cattle cults were widespread and prominent, as
is indicated by the emblems of nomes VI and X-XII (Kees 1961,
p. 30; Montet 1957, pp. 89 ff., 119 ff., 129 ff.; Helck 1974, pp.
151 ff.);

2.   Old Kingdom reliefs show great herds of cattle in the
Delta (see Klebs 1915, p. 60); and sheep were important in at least
nomes XV and XVI (Kees 1961, pp. 37, 91 f.);

3.   The Kamose Stela (17th Dynasty) records Theban grazing
rights in the Delta wetlands (James 1973), and the chief archi-
tect of Thutmosis I kept herds in the Delta (see Sethe 1906, § 73);

4.   Ramses III brought five great herds of captured Libyan cattle into the Delta (see Breasted 1906, pp. 119 ff.);

   5. Ptolemaic records show that cattle raising was important in nomes III, VI, and XI (Montet 1957, pp. 66 f., 94 f., 135);
   6. Cattle pastoralists of nome VI revolted in both Roman
and Arab times (Kees 1961, p. 30).
Yet the Delta was far from a pastoral landscape. Many nomes have
no documented links with cattle cults or herding, and instead nomes
III and XVII were traditionally renowned for their garden agriculture and orchards (Montet 1957, pp. 66, 115 f.). Furthermore,
important wines were produced in nomes III, XIV, and XIX, with
other vineyards in nomes IX, XII, and XVI (Strabo XVII:1-14;
Gardiner 1947, pp. 235 f.; Hayes 1951, pp. 85 ff.; Kees 1961, pp.
81 f., 185; Montet 1957, pp. 66, 182). This all suggests that
specialized forms of agriculture were far more prominent than in
the Nile Valley, while pastoralism retained much of its prehistoric significance, at least through the Ptolemaic era. A combination of subsistence farming, herding, and commercial plan-
tations can therefore be envisaged.

   Political and military organization of the eastern Delta was
the New Kingdom's response to the earlier invasion of the Hyksos
from Asia. New centers of gravity on the Delta margins led to
increased status for peripheral cult centers and the resulting
creation of nome XVII by the 18th Dynasty, and of nomes XVIII-
XX in the 22nd Dynasty (Bietak 1975, pp. 149 ff.). Concomitant
economic development, mainly along the western and eastern Delta
margins, is also indicated by eleven towns first verified in the
Ramessid period (fig. 4). Consequently, the Delta population
may have doubled during the course of the Old Kingdom, and again
during the early Ramessid era, when the absolute level but not
the relative density possibly began to rival that of the Nile
Valley.

   The greatest population increase came even later, however.
The Ptolemaic period saw the demographic and political center
of gravity shift permanently to Lower Egypt. Over thirty-five
new towns are verified for the interval 950 B.C.-A.D. 600, when
much of the northern marsh country, particularly the Mareotis
(Shafei 1952; Bernand 1971, pp. 103 f.), was first settled (fig.
4), in no small part facilitated by the negative oscillation of
sea level at this time. In addition, the Mediterranean littoral
and its sea harbors[10] now first achieved special importance

   10. Canopus (Pegu) is, however, verified since the 12th Dynasty (see Porter and Moss 1934, p. 2; Montet 1957, p. 72). Both
Canopus and Alexandria were sited on partly submerged ridges of

(Kemp and O'Connor 1974; Montet 1957, p. 73; Bernand 1971, pp. 316 f.). Notwithstanding, marshes and related big-game hunting[11] remained prominent in nomes VII, XIV, and XVI-XVII throughout historical times (Montet 1957, pp. 73 f., 116, 143, 170, 200 ff.; Kees 1961, pp. 32 f.; Niemeyer 1936, pp. 28 f.), while the importance of fishing in nomes VII, XV, and XVI (see Montet 1957, pp. 73 f., 140, 143 f.; Kees 1961, pp. 92 f.) was probably related to coastal waterways much as in recent times (Niemeyer 1936, pp. 28, 68 f.; Simons 1968, p. 184).

It would appear that Delta settlement proceeded in stages: the filling out of the southern and central Delta during the Old Kingdom, the development of the desert margins and the Asiatic periphery during Ramessid times, followed by colonization of the northern Delta, the Mareotis, and the Alexandrian littoral under the Saites and Ptolemies. Although the Delta must have been fundamentally suitable for settlement, excessive water and possibly endemic malaria may have proved to be inhibiting factors that could only be compensated for by technological improvements. The probable demographic development in response to the expansion of cultivated lands and the intensification of land use outlined is presented in table 4. It is reasonable to suppose that population density continued to grow in Roman and Byzantine times, until a succession of coastal disasters that were related to subsidence of the northernmost Delta by autocompaction, storm incursions of a Mediterranean Sea gradually rising in the first millennium A.D., and occasional Nile disasters by exceptionally high floods. This period of readjustment, and gradual abandonment of the Delta fringe to water and salt, appears to have extended from the fourth through the fifteenth century A.D. (see Niemeyer 1936, pp. 21 ff.; Shafei 1952; Hamdan 1961; Bernand 1971, pp. 117 ff.; Sestini, forthcoming). The single, major catastrophe may have occurred in A.D. 961.

---

cemented beach sand.

    11. Most of the big-game hunting of the 18th-Dynasty pharaohs appears to have taken place in Nubia or Syria, but Amenhotep III's claim to ninety-six wild cattle in a single hunting expedition was probably made out of Memphis and presumably refers to marshes amid the sand islands of the east-central Delta (contra Drioton 1947; see also Desroches-Noblecourt 1950).

The Desert Oases and the Steppes

Population estimates for the non-Egyptian peoples west and
east of the Nile would allow an appreciation of the nature of the
desert frontiers. Obviously there is no direct data base but more
recent figures do at least allow discussion. According to the
1882 census, the first of its kind in the Libyan Oases (see H.J.L.
Beadnell, in Willcocks 1904, chap. 5, for a summary description),
the combined, sedentary population of Siwa, Bahariya, Farafra,
Dakhla, and Kharga was 30,687 (Toussoun 1932). In 1927, when the
total cultivated land was 80 sq km, the number of inhabitants had
risen to 35,514 (Toussoun 1932), a population density of 444/sq
km, which represents a response to development of the artesian
water resources (see Murray 1951, 1955) that had begun in the
1860s (see Niemeyer 1936, pp. 81 ff.).

It is, therefore, doubtful whether there were more than 35,000
inhabitants in the oases during the most intensive phase of Greco-
Roman development (see Fakhry 1973a, 1973b; 1974a, 1974b). Furthermore, it is probable that the Libyco-Berber population of the
desert oases in earlier times (see Hayes 1964, pp. 225 ff.) never
exceeded 15,000 or 20,000, also not during moister climatic intervals. Although even the 1966 census provides no ready estimate
of the pastoral population of the western coastal steppe, or Marmarica, it was somewhat less than one-third of the total population
of 97,477 (see Fakhry 1973a, p. 11). The nomads of the Red Sea Hill
country today number perhaps a few thousand.

These data and arguments suggest that the total "desert"
population of Dynastic Egypt was substantially under 50,000, even
at times of optimal climate and groundwater supply (see table 4).
This implies that only small groups of at most a few hundred raiders
ever threatened the Egyptian frontier at any one time. More effective would have been the intrusion of seminomadic squatters onto
the floodplain and its peripheries: their 1882 counterpart pur-
portedly numbered about 200,000 "nomadic" beduin, almost 3% of
the floodplain population (see Boinet 1886, C. Baer 1969, p. 3)--
concentrated along the Delta margins, in the Faiyum, and in northwestern Egypt (see Niemeyer 1936, pp. 22 f., 78 ff.). Consequently, shortly before 950 B.C., there may well have been several times
as many Libyans living in the Delta and Nile Valley than there
were in the Marmarica and Libyan Oases combined. This confirms
the impression that the power base for the accession of the Libyan
dynasties (945-715 B.C.) was within the alluvial lands of Egypt,

among the descendants of settlers who arrived a century or two earlier (see Černý 1965; Kitchen 1973, pp. 245, 345 ff.).

8

PERSPECTIVES ON SETTLEMENT PATTERNING

The settlement macropatterns and demographic changes of ancient Egypt bring a number of realizations and problems into focus.

For one, the environmental contrasts of the valley, oasis, and delta landscapes are strikingly reflected in the historical trajectory of each region. Strabo had noted the distinctiveness of the several Egyptian landscapes during his visit, and Herodotus, the first outsider to ponder the historical ensemble, recognized the basic differences in the economic development of each. Both had the advantage of external perspective and of time, and were therefore able to draw explicit attention to features glossed over or unrecognized by the Egyptian scribes and chroniclers. The Egyptian historiographers were obsessed with ritual and the cyclic, repetitive nature of events, ignoring many aspects of the economic plane,[1] and viewed their internal universe in terms of the symbolic dualism of Upper and Lower Egypt, or in relation to the shrines of local deities. An equally two-dimensional but diachronic model of sequential Old, Middle, and New kingdoms was adopted by nineteenth-century historians of ancient Egypt. This monolithic concept and the ingrained assumption of Egyptian conservatism has tended to obscure many of the implications of the very substantial body of research.

---

1. This is not to deny the existence of an extensive corpus of economic data in the Egyptian records. However, by the standards of Mesopotamia, the relevant Egyptian materials are incomplete and less satisfactory as a source for statistical information (see Janssen 1975a, chap. 4).

If anything, the Egyptian record speaks for repeated innovations in organizational skills and technology, an essentially
flexible system of repeated ecological adjustment, and a remarkably
complex and large-scale progression of economic development. If
local irrigation systems in Mesopotamia were at times more pre-
cocious, they were also far more ephemeral. And the European
domain of the Caesars was underdeveloped by Egyptian standards even
in the second century A.D. Egypt is therefore the prime example of
an irrigation civilization, whether or not it conformed with
Wittfogel's (1938, 1957, p. 344) particular definition of a
"hydraulic society" or with the political structure of "Oriental
despotism" (see also Balandier 1970, pp. 144 f.).

As Cowgill (1975a, 1975b) and Hassan (1974, forthcoming)
have pointed out, it has become unduly fashionable for archeologists and anthropologists to see population pressures and ecological stress as "prime movers" in stimulating intensification
of agricultural production and other technical and social innovations. To examine here the theoretical frameworks of population
growth in historical Egypt would lead to circular arguments, since
our speculations on demographic development were explicitly linked
to technological change. Nonetheless, a good case can be made for
specific ecological controls over actual population levels and
theoretical carrying capacity. It remains to consider the striking anomaly of Egyptian agriculture in the context of the Roman
Empire or of other African floodplains with comparable physical
attributes. There is, of course, no simple answer to the underlying question of why some populations grow repeatedly while
others remain stable in comparable settings or with similar resources. But it is imperative to probe more deeply into the
spatial distribution of population that was peculiar to early
civilization in Egypt.

The evidence developed here shows that the Egyptian population was most dense in the south, between Aswan and Qift, and
again in the north, between the Faiyum entrance and the head of
the Delta. At a later time the Faiyum itself became another
high-density area. But the broad floodplain in between, and the
vast Delta itself, remained thinly settled throughout the Dynastic
era. In part, location theory would explicate that the growth of
national administrative centers at Memphis and Luxor-Karnak should
encourage agricultural intensification and concentrations of
population in their proximity. Quite apart from economic incen-

tives, such as transportation costs, it is apparent that social
and political factors (see Trigger 1972) also favored the dominance
of a few royal residences and the gradual decline of other, provincial centers.

But the Delta case suggests that other determinants were also
involved. There is a visual relationship between narrow floodplain segments and high population density that transcends the
hinterland of the key national centers. This can be expressed
in quantitative terms, for the valley proper, by determining the
length of the Nile channel in proportion to the area of each
nome. A linear river frontage is given for each nome in table 3,
adjusted for adjacent nomes on opposite riverbanks by halving
common frontage. A ratio of river frontage to area is then cal-
culated (table 3), and plotted with respect to nome population
density (fig. 14). The results confirm that, despite a great number of political and ecological variables, and some local problems
of incomplete representation, density was an inverse function of
floodplain width. In all probability this situation reflected
the uneven nature of early agricultural colonization of the
alluvial lands, a view implicitly favored by the apparent Predynastic settlement gap in the valley north of Asyut (see discussion
in Kaiser 1961). Only in Coptic times did the population density
of the broader floodplain segments increase (Butzer 1960a) to
relative proportions comparable to those of today (see fig. 12).

By way of explanation, agricultural settlements should initially have been spaced fairly evenly along the Nile. The wider
the floodplain, the larger the hinterland available for exploitation and for satellite settlements from the original river-edge
sites. Mechanically, the narrow floodplain segments would "fill
out" first, other conditions being equal. More specifically, in
terms of Carneiro's (1972) formula, the time required for the
population of a circumscribed area to bring all arable land
into the agricultural cycle is a function of the area of arable
land, the size of an average subsistence plot, the pattern of
cultivation and fallow, the initial population, and the population growth rate. Carneiro further argues that as carrying
capacity is reached and land shortages become acute, there is
forceful acquisition of territory, leading inevitably to fusion
of villages into chiefdoms, "and so on up the scale of political
development" (Carneiro 1972, p. 69). This process of unification is only thought to be inhibited when population pressure

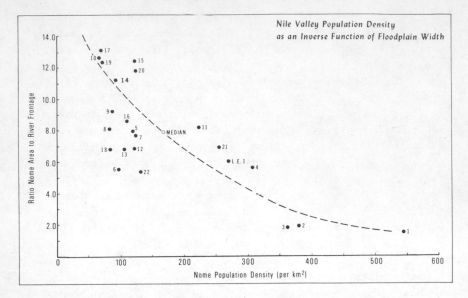

Fig. 14.--Nile valley population density during Dynastic times in relation to floodplain width. Numbers refer to Upper Egyptian nomes; L.E. 1 is the Memphite nome.

promotes intensification of cultivation. Both principles should operate best in an environmentally circumscribed area, such as a riverine oasis.

Despite any superficial appeal, neither argument can be readily applied to the Nile Valley. The concept of "nuclear" versus "peripheral" areas, defined by population density, is easily transferred. Thus the nucleus in nomes I-V was restricted from centrifugal expansion by desert to the west and east, and by the narrow, discontinuous floodplain of Nubia to the south. Northward expansion and colonization would be logical. Similarly, the Memphite nucleus had the possibility of northward expansion into the Delta or southward, to an ultimate confrontation with Upper Egypt. Nonetheless some three millennia elapsed between the political unification of Egypt and the "filling out" of the broad, intermediate floodplain expanses and of the delta plain. Two explanations can be offered: one ecological and the other social.

The natural flood basins of the Nile are small and therefore easily manageable where the floodplain is narrow, but they are large and difficult to operate where the flats are extensive.

Even the modern basins, as artificially subdivided, continue
to show similar proportions, with those of former nomes I-VII
less than one-third the size of those of the more northerly provinces. A similar contrast applies to the broad, northern floodplain, to the west of the Nile, where basins average four times the
size of the east bank (see Willcocks 1889, table 16). It was
therefore much easier to implement artificial irrigation in the
far south, and on the eastern bank of the Nile (contra Willcocks 1904, pp. 65 f.), where basins did not require transverse
dikes and where basins filled and emptied like clockwork under
natural conditions. This may well explain the preferential location
of the nome capitals on the east bank (fig. 11). On the other
hand, the great, low-gradient west-bank basins of nomes VIII-
XX, even where subidvided by seasonal Nile branches, required advanced skills, considerable manpower, and greater social organization to bring under control. The persistent "underpopulation"
of these same nomes until at least the Ptolemaic era may well reflect on the same technological impediments that slowed down
the development of the Delta. In fact, O'Connor (1972a) has argued that extensive farming or pastoralism was characteristic of
these underpopulated nomes even in late Ramessid times.

The second factor appears to have been regional particularism,
presumably based originally on tribal identities, and dimly reflected over the millennia by the pliable but persistent nome
structure of the Nile Valley and Delta. Helck (1974, pp. 199 ff.)
argues that a minimum of sixteen Upper and ten Lower Egyptian
nomes antedate the 3rd Dynasty, and Edwards (1971) identifies
several of the primeval nome standards of both regions on mace-
heads and palettes dating from shortly before and after the unification of Egypt ca. 3050 B.C. The nomes probably find their
origins among natural basin-irrigation units of the evolving agricultural landscape and a continuing link with the regulation of
irrigation is suggested by the Old Kingdom title of $^c\underline{d}$-mr, "he
who cuts the canals," applied to governors and certain other regional
administrators in Lower Egypt (see Fischer 1969, pp. 9 ff.).

Despite several reorganizations and redefinitions of their
political and administrative functions, the same basic nomes
survived the centralization of the Old Kingdom with distinctive
secular and religious administrations (Fischer 1969, pp. 18 ff.),
to display at least a semblance of regional autonomy in politics,
pottery traditions (see Arnold, forthcoming; also O'Connor 1974),

and even literary style (Fischer, forthcoming) during the First
Intermediate Period. The Middle Kingdom pharaohs, who ultimately
eliminated the power of the nomarchs (see O'Connor 1974; Helck
1974, p. 202), saw fit to concentrate their own activities in the
"virgin lands" of the Faiyum, much as the Old Kingdom ruling
elite was primarily engaged in developmental activities in the
Delta, an area that appears to have been very closely attached to
the central government. Although circumstantial as an argument,
it is probable that at least the traditional Upper Egyptian nomes
maintained a degree of social identity well into the Middle Kingdom
so that, except for times of chaos (see Bell 1971), they served
to inhibit spontaneous internal colonization or government-spon-
sored resettlements across nome boundaries. This factor may well
provide a partial explanation for the disjunct centers of population density that persisted throughout the Dynastic period.

    The degree to which nome identity was subsequently eroded dur-
ing the New Kingdom and later is uncertain (Yoyotte 1959), but
Helck (1974, pp. 108, 114 f., 119, 127) believes that several
nomes were subsumed into larger fiscal and administrative units.
Veterans, officers, and foreign mercenaries were allocated considerable lands in select areas (see Gardiner 1948, pp. 79 ff.;
O'Connor 1972a), an indication that internal colonization on a
relatively large scale was among the practices of the New Kingdom pharaohs. A more limited nome autonomy can also be inferred
from the fact that the great majority of upper-class provincial
tombs belonged to holders of national office, as opposed to local
officials, such as mayors.

    Thus significant demographic changes, presumably including
strong trends to urbanization, as well as rural emigration outward from the densely populated nomes, appear to have been under
way by the time of the New Kingdom Empire. In the absence of political and social constraints, the surplus population of the narrow,
southern floodplain nomes must have begun to spill over into the
broad expanses of the valley north of Abydos, inasfar as the available irrigation technology would allow. This offers a reasonable
explanation for the increasing number of larger towns in that
area toward the end of the New Kingdom. Such an interpretation
is preferable to O'Connor's (1972a, 1972b) view that these larger
towns reflected defensive regroupings in response to political
disintegration and resulting instability.

In Ptolemaic times the entire administration of the floodplain was reorganized (see Butzer 1960a). A set of new *nomoi*,
corresponding approximately to the traditional nomes in location,
were created as standardized administrative subdivisions, directly
responsible to the central government in Alexandria. Each nome
metropolis, situated on the Nile or linked to it by a designated
harbor, served as the political and cultural focus for the
middle-echelon bureaucracy and colonies of veterans, both groups
overwhelmingly of Greek origin. During the subsequent centuries
a number of large urban centers developed in Upper Egypt, competing
with the traditional centers of Luxor-Karnak and Memphis. At the
same time the process of "filling out" was completed, as the many
new Hellenistic and Byzantine-Coptic settlements in northern Upper Egypt show. By the time of the Arab conquest a totally different pattern of urban centers and relative population densities
is apparent in the Nile Valley. Despite the fluctuations of absolute population, this pattern persisted into modern times.

In other words, the spatial organization of Egyptian settlement has for manifold reasons been linked with the nomes since
late Predynastic times. These nomes, as basic territorial en-
tities, originally had socio-economic as well as ecologic over-
tones, but then became increasingly administrative in nature.
At times of centralization the nome capitals declined, only to
regain stature during the centuries of weak national government.
Regional particularism also was not the same in New Kingdom or
Ptolemaic times as it had been during the First Intermediate Period.
However, the continuing prominence of the majority of the traditional
nome capitals in the urban hierarchy argues that certain economic, religious, or administrative functions were maintained in
most instances. Consequently, even though their original social
identity had been lost, and the nome scheme reduced to a formal
and stylized geographical overlay, the nomes continued to have
real effects on the central-place hierarchy of Egypt. In my
opinion, the peculiar pervasiveness of the nome structure across
four millennia profoundly affected the development of macrosettlement patterns in Egypt.

9

CONCLUSIONS AND IMPLICATIONS

This study has attempted to focus on an array of problems that have received only limited explicit attention by Egyptologists, but for which they have nonetheless carefully assembled a wealth of fundamental data. I have alternatingly taken the stance of the anthropologist or geographer, in order to articulate the problems differently and to search for fresh and, wherever possible, more broadly based explanations. Furthermore, I have chosen a discursive approach with limited documentation, in preference to a more limited but tightly argued case. Many of my suggestions are deliberately speculative, in the hope that they may provoke more painstaking research by Egyptologists, particularly in the field of economic history. With these qualifications borne in mind, the major conclusions can be summarized.

1. The Nile floodplain and delta are free-draining, seasonally inundated alluvial surfaces that have marked the focus of human settlement since Paleolithic times. Most settlement sites of ten to twenty millennia ago were already situated on the immediate banks of the Nile, and desert-edge settlements or cemeteries have frequently been misinterpreted as steps in a comparatively late agricultural colonization of the valley. In fact, drainage was no general prerequisite to cultivation, and artificial irrigation was an option desirable only to increase acreage and equalize year-to-year productivity of the naturally irrigated flood basins. Local rains were of some ecological significance at first, and Nile flood levels were also substantially higher during Predynastic times. However seasonal grazing resources in the deserts were negligible since the early Old Kingdom, and the Nile floods became the only environmental parameter of note. These floods declined during the course of the Old Kingdom, and the First Intermediate Period

saw Nile failures of catastrophic proportions. Flood levels rose
during the Middle Kingdom, becoming exceptionally high for at least
a while, and then declined precipitously during later Ramessid
times. Good floods appear to have been the rule under the Saites
and Ptolemies. In the Delta, the temporary eustatic rises of Mediterranean sea level ca. 3000 and 1200 B.C. appear to have been
offset by strong Nile flood discharge and higher sedimentation
rates, while continued alluviation during the lower sea level oscil-
lations ca. 2200 and 300 B.C. favored emergence of the northernmost Delta.

   2. Intensive gathering activities, suggestive of reaping
and grinding of wild grains, are already apparent in Upper Egypt
and Nubia among some Late Paleolithic cultural groups as early
as 12,500 B.C. Although the Epi-Paleolithic archeological inventory offers no direct information to this effect, indigenous domestication of cattle and local seed grasses may have been
attempted in Egypt well before 5000 B.C., and experimentation
with local cultigens and animal domesticates did indeed persist
into the Old Kingdom. It is possible that broad-spectrum hunting-
and-gathering subsistence on the Nile floodplain was sufficiently
successful so that exotic cultigens and domesticated animals were
"resisted" until 5200 B.C., and even thereafter accepted only slow-
ly and incompletely. The result was a Predynastic culture of
mixed roots and considerable individuality. Cattle and goat pastoralism far outweighed cultivation of emmer, barley, and flax,
while considerable reliance was still placed on fishing, fowling,
and big-game hunting.

   3. Artificial irrigation, including deliberate flooding and
draining by sluice gates, and water contained by longitudinal
and transverse dikes, was established by the 1st Dynasty. Con-
trolled irrigation was easiest among the smaller flood basins of
southern Upper Egypt and further north, on the east bank. In
these areas, crop cultivation steadily increased at the expense
of pastoral activities and the remaining tracts of "natural"
vegetation. In this way an arid climate was more than compensated for by highly productive soils and conditioned by the exotic
water supply of a riverine oasis. Development of the larger
basins required considerably more experience and, above all,
a massive input of labor. Then, as in more recent times, the
maintenance of this rudimentary system of flood irrigation, gov-
erned by a powerful river, further required large-scale coopera-

tion in the regular opening or closing of the dikes, and particularly at times of exceptionally high floods. Summer garden crops or cultivation of the high-lying levees were impossible without lift irrigation, first mechanized by the introduction of the lever or shaduf during the 18th Dynasty and then
revolutionized by the waterwheel or saqiya in early Ptolemaic
times. Even thereafter, summer or flood crops were planted largely on a horticultural basis, requiring as they did considerable
application of fertilizer. Examination of the impact of strong
or deficient floods on such a rudimentary and locally organized
irrigation system suggests that the apparent redistributory and
managerial functions of the local temples, at least during the New
Kingdom, would have been of paramount significance in coping with
the vagaries of the river. Until such a time, periodic deficient
floods kept population levels well below carrying capacity, particularly during times of incompetent government. Altogether the
economic history of ancient Egypt was primarily one of continuous
ecological readjustment to a variable water supply, combined with
repeated efforts to intensify or expand land use in order to increase productivity.

4. The available Dynastic settlement record has been reconstructed and utilized to estimate crude, relative population densities in the different nomes of the Nile Valley, and to suggest
concentrations in the narrower floodplain segments of the far
south and far north. It can be argued that intensive utilization
of the intervening section of broader floodplain was rendered difficult by the great size of the natural flood basins. Furthermore, it is possible that internal colonization was inhibited, at
least through Middle Kingdom times, by a nome structure originally based on tribal subdivisions among the Nile flood basins.
Only in the New Kingdom did government resettlement of veterans
and mercenaries, and more spontaneous emigration from the densely
populated, smaller, southern nomes, begin to fill out the broad
floodplain north of Abydos, a process finally completed in Coptic
times. The Faiyum provides a special case, with some regulation of lake level and a first stage of colonization achieved in
the Middle Kingdom. It remained for the Ptolemies to reduce the
lake to a much smaller size, yet establishing an efficient, large-
scale network of radial irrigation that allowed a trebling of
the cultivated land. In the Delta, internal colonization contributed to complex agricultural development of the southern and

central sectors during the Old Kingdom, of the desert margins
and the Asiatic periphery in Ramessid times, and of the northern
marshes and coasts under the Ptolemies. Each stage of Delta development may have doubled the regional population, until the
demographic center of gravity shifted from the Nile Valley to the
Delta in Hellenistic times.

    5. A multitiered economy is already suggested by the monu-
mental architecture of the Early Dynastic period, and complex social
stratification in the urban sector is abundantly evident from
the written records of the Old Kingdom (Baer 1960). Yet the Mesopotamian model of rapid population growth leading to greater competition for water, increased labor efficiency, intensified irrigation, a more intricate division of labor, social stratification, and, ultimately, state superstructures (R. Adams 1972)
cannot be documented for Egypt.

    Competition for water was never an issue, except at the
local level, since whatever was done in any one natural flood
basin, it did not deprive the next basins downstream of their
direct access to the Nile. In a radial irrigation system (see
fig. 6B) water inputs were artificially regulated at each dis-
tributional node, allowing for serious potential conflicts. On
the Egyptian floodplain and delta, cooperation was essential only
within natural flood basins, in the general maintenance and effective interdigitation of the artificial subbasins. The absence of written regulations from Dynastic Egypt suggests that
water legislation was not overly complex, and that it was administered locally. The fact that many other aspects of civil
and criminal law were codified repeatedly in response to new
economic or social situations argues that water legislation belonged within the oldest oral traditions of common law. It further implies that such legislation accumulated in prehistoric
times, prior to the establishment of any centralized political
superstructure, yet required no formal modification in later
millennia.

    All the evidence converges to suggest that, at the social and
administrative level, flood control and irrigation were and continued to be managed locally, by the mass input of the total,
able-bodied rural population of a basin unit, much like during
the Mameluke era (see G. Baer 1969, chap. 2). Most Egyptians
continued to live the traditional way of life in villages and small
centers, unlike Mesopotamia, where the development of civiliza-

tion drew a high percentage of the rural population into urban
spheres (Trigger, forthcoming). Even in the rural Egypt of the
Mamelukes, division of labor and class distinctions were minimal
in a subsistence economy based on basin irrigation; it was the
cash crop production of perennial irrigation that allowed certain
rural groups to effect a new economic and social differentiation
that dissolved the village community as a cohesive social unit
(G. Baer 1969, pp. 28 f.). Although Old Kingdom Egypt was strongly centralized in terms of its political superstructure, there is
reason to assume that the infrastructure, at least in Upper Egypt,
continued to function on more traditional lines via a number of
indirect agents and agencies that mediated between Memphis and the
local communities.[1] It is significant that the plethora of Old
Kingdom titles provides no evidence for a centralized, bureau-
cratic apparatus that might have served to administer irrigation
at the national, regional, or local level (see K. Baer 1960 and
personal communication). It seems, therefore, that ecological problems were preeminently handled at the local level, at least until
the opening up of the Faiyum in the Middle Kingdom. The development of a professional full-time bureaucracy must therefore be
related to a different social impetus. In other words, there is
no direct causal relationship between hydraulic agriculture and
the development of the Pharaonic political structure and society.

      6. One might argue that hydraulic agriculture provided the
indispensable economic resource base for the complex, state-cen-
tered society that had emerged in the form of the Old Kingdom, yet

---

      1. Pharaoh's power in the Old Kingdom appears to have
been virtually absolute, but the implementation of central
authority is less clear. So, for example, the royal estates scattered along the length of the Nile Valley during the 3rd and 4th
dynasties may reflect on the personal nature of the king's original
power base in Upper Egypt, and may further attest to a late prehistoric system of periodic royal visitations to collect tribute
personally from otherwise autonomous sociopolitical units--analo-
gous to similar practices in classical Axum or medieval Ethiopia
(see Kobishchanov 1966, chap. 3). Similarly, the apparent residence and burial of most Old Kingdom nomarchs and mayors in the
shadow of the king served to channel authority to the provinces
while inhibiting separatist tendencies. In combination with the
limited range of documented titles of appointment related to
national (in contrast to local or regional) functions, these features can be used to suggest that the central administration was
limited in its scope. Even in the New Kingdom the persistent
and prominent role of the temples as an adjunct of the state
(see Kemp 1972a) argues for a relatively decentralized system of
fiscal and judicial administration.

high economic productivity is essential to any complex society.
More distinctive may be the socio-economic anchoring of the Egyptian nomes into the explicit ecological framework of the riverine
oasis. These primeval nomes appear to have provided the necessary
political infrastructure for the military ventures that over
several generations of strife led to the unification of Egypt. In
this sense Pharaonic civilization remains inconceivable without
its ecological determinants, but not by the linear causality model
of stress → irrigation → managerial bureaucracy → despotic control.

      These salient points and conclusions have implications that
go well beyond the Egyptian case.

      The fundamental interrelationships between man and his
environment in the Egyptian floodplain influenced the evolution
of land use patterns, the development of irrigation, the spatial
distribution of settlements, and, last but not least, set a
demographic ratio between actual population and theoretical carrying capacity. The details are not necessarily understood, but
the evidence that this was indeed so militates against the fashionable trend to view the origins of civilization and of urbanism
solely in sociological and political terms. It also cautions
against economic interpretations of early floodplain civilizations that overemphasize craft specializations, redistribution of
raw materials and finished products, and the emergence of multitiered societies, to the practical exclusion of the highly dynamic
variables that condition floodplain ecosystems.

      The Egyptian example provides some unexpected insights
into the emergence of an irrigation civilization that not only
caution against oversimplification of the variables. It is possible, in my view, not only to overlook the complexity of historical processes but for this very reason to grossly misunder-
stand the functional mechanisms involved. I doubt that the
Egyptian pattern elucidated here is applicable to other irrigation civilizations, but the conclusions diverge sufficiently
from existing assumptions and paradigms to argue a need for
analogous investigations in other regions.

      For my own, long-standing interest in diachronic man-
land interrelationships, the Egyptian example showed an un-
expected continuity in environmental exploitation strategies between prehistoric communities of the Pleistocene and the much
more complex and sophisticated cultures of historical times. Ad-

mittedly this is a matter of perspective, but to me the differences
lie at the level of technology, that is, tactics, and intensity,
that is, degree. The rationale of settlement location and
specialized resource utilization in a circumscribed ecosystem of
unusual productivity remained much the same.

The existence of written records, no matter how oblique,
adds an exquisitely human dimension that is painfully lacking in
prehistoric contexts. It would be exaggerated to claim that the
Egyptian literary corpus explains the "land ethic" of that culture. Yet the brief glimpses that it provides into human activities, suffering, and implicit attitudes can never be replicated
by any degree of purely archeological research addressed to prehistoric communities. This again should serve as a caveat to
the widespread expectation among archeologists that prehistoric
lifeways can indeed be reconstructed with sufficiently improved
methodologies. I feel strongly that the Egyptian example cautions
against models that optimistically seek to (over)interpret prehistoric settlement systems.

Finally, it needs to be said that the Egyptian pictorial
record, unique in its own right, is crucial to much of the argument presented here. Thematically it includes not only fauna and
flora, but the rural landscape, technology, the agricultural
cycle, and, above all, the human view. This perspective among
some 3,000 years of mobile art, tomb reliefs or frescoes, and
other visual representations from Egypt provides a rich tapestry
of information and impressions that complement the written records.
The two lines of evidence generally corroborate each other and provide added dimensions, as well as a more complete picture. For
these reasons it is important that more archeologists develop
an appreciation for the potential of prehistoric rock art, particularly in the Sahara. For all too long, most of the best archeological methodologists have scorned rock art for its subjectivity
as an artifact of research. In fact, it is the very subjectivity
of this peculiarly human form of expression that can potentially
add invaluable dimensions to the otherwise mute physical and archeological record.

BIBLIOGRAPHY

Adams, R. M. 1965. *Land behind Baghdad: A history of settlement on the Diyala Plains*. Chicago: University of Chicago
Press. 197 pp.

---. 1966. *The evolution of urban society: Early Mesopotamia
and prehispanic Mexico*. Chicago: Aldine Pub. Co. 199 pp.

---. 1972. Demography and the "urban revolution" in lowland Mesopotamia. In *Population growth: Anthropological implications*,
ed. B. Spooner, pp. 60-63. Cambridge: M.I.T. Press.

---. 1974. Anthropological perspectives on ancient trade. *Current
Anthropol*. 15:239-58.

Adams, R. M., and Nissen, H. J. 1972. *The Uruk countryside:
The natural setting of urban societies*. Chicago: University of Chicago Press. 241 pp.

Adams, W. Y. 1965. Sudan Antiquities Service excavations at
Meinarti, 1963-64. *Kush* 13:148-77.

---. 1967. Continuity and change in Nubian cultural history.
Sudan Notes Rec. 48:1-32.

Anderson, J. E. 1968. Late Paleolithic skeletal remains from
Nubia. In *The Prehistory of Nubia*, ed. F. Wendorf, pp. 996-
1040. Dallas: Southern Methodist University Press.

Angel, J. L. 1972. Ecology and population in the Eastern Mediterranean. *World Archaeol*. 4:88-105.

Arkell, A. J., and Ucko, P. J. 1965. Review of Predynastic development in the Nile Valley. *Current Anthropol*. 6:145-66.

Arnold, Dorothea. Forthcoming. The study and historical significance of Egyptian pottery. In *Ancient Egypt: Problems of
history, sources and methods*, eds. D. O'Connor and D. Redford. Warminster, England: Aris & Phillips, Ltd.

113

Asselberghs, Henri. 1961. *Chaos en Beheersing: Documenten uit aeneolitisch Egypte*. Leiden: E. J. Brill. 342 pp. and 104 pl.

Attia, J. I. 1954. *Deposits in the Nile Valley and the Delta*. Cairo: Geological Survey of Egypt, Government Press. 356 pp.

Badawy, Alexander. 1954-68. *A history of Egyptian architecture*. Vol. 1. 1954. *From the earliest times to the end of the Old Kingdom*. Cairo: Urwand. 212 pp. Vol. 2. 1966. *The Middle Kingdom*. Berkeley and Los Angeles: University of California Press. 272 pp. Vol. 3. 1968. *The Empire*. Berkeley and Los Angeles: University of California Press. 548 pp.

Baer, Gabriel. 1969. *Studies in the social history of modern Egypt*. Chicago: University of Chicago Press. 259 pp.

Baer, Klaus. 1960. *Rank and title in the Old Kingdom: The structure of the Egyptian administration in the 5th and 6th dynasties*. Chicago: University of Chicago Press. 310 pp.

———. 1962. The low price of land in ancient Egypt. *J. Am. Res. Cent. Egypt* 1:25-42.

———. 1963. An 11th-Dynasty farmer's letters to his family. *J. Am. Oriental Soc.* 83:1-19.

———. N.d. Land and water in Ancient Egypt. Unpublished manuscript.

Balandier, Georges. 1970. *Political anthropology*. New York: Pantheon Books, Inc. 214 pp.

Ball, John. 1932. The *Déscription de l'Égypte* and the course of the Nile between Isna and Girga. *Bull. Inst. Egypte* 14:127-39

———. 1939. *Contributions to the geography of Egypt*. Cairo: Survey of Egypt, Government Press. 308 pp.

———. 1942. *Egypt in the classical geographers*. Cairo: Survey of Egypt, Government Press. 203 pp.

Barker, H.; Burleigh, R.; and Meeks, N. 1971. British Museum natural radiocarbon measurements VII. *Radiocarbon* 13:157-88.

Batrawi, Ahmed. 1945-46. The racial history of Egypt and Nubia. *J. Roy. Anthropol. Inst.* 75:81-101; 76:131-56.

Baumann, B. B. 1960. The botanical aspects of ancient Egyptian embalming and burial. *Econ. Botany* 14:84-104.

Baumgartel, E. J. 1947-60. *The cultures of prehistoric Egypt*. 2 vols. London: Oxford University Press. 123+164 pp.

———. 1966. Scorpion and rosette and the fragment of the large Hierakonpolis mace head. *Z. Ägyptische Sprache Altertumskunde* 92:9-14.

———. 1970. Predynastic Egypt. In *Cambridge Ancient History*, rev. ed., 1, pt. 1:463-97.

Beckerath, Jürgen von. 1966. The Nile level records at Karnak and their importance for the history of the Libyan period. *J. Am. Res. Cent. Egypt* 5:43-55.

Bell, Barbara. 1970. The oldest records of the Nile floods. *Geograph. J.* 136:569-73.

———. 1971. The Dark Ages in ancient history: I. The First Dark Age in Egypt. *Am. J. Archaeol.* 75:1-26.

———. 1975. Climate and the history of Egypt: The Middle Kingdom. *Am. J. Archaeol.* 79:223-69.

Bender, Barbara. 1975. *Farming in prehistory.* London: John Baker. 268 pp.

Bernand, André. 1971. Le Delta égyptien d'après les textes grecs: I. Les confins libyques. *Mem. Inst. Fr. Archéol. Orientale* 41:1-1133.

Berry, A. C.; Berry, R. J.; and Ucko, P. J. 1967. Genetical change in ancient Egypt. *Man* 2:551-68.

Berry, Leonard. 1960. *Large-scale alluvial islands in the White Nile*, pp. 14-19. Khartum: Hydrobiological Research Unit, University of Khartum.

Bietak, Manfred. 1966. Ausgrabungen in Sayala-Nubien 1961-65: Denkmäler der C-Gruppe und der Pan-Gräber Kultur. *Denkschr. Akad. Wiss. Österreich Phil. Hist. Kl.* 92:1-100.

———. 1968. Studien zur Chronologie der nubischen C-Gruppe. *Denkschr. Österreich. Akad. Wiss. Phil. Hist. Kl.* 97:1-188.

———. 1975. Tell el-Dabá II; der Fundort im Rahmen einer archäologisch-geographischen Untersuchung über das ägyptische Ostdelta. Untersuchungen der Zweigstelle Kairo des Österreichischen Archäologischen Institutes I. *Österreich. Akad. Wiss. Denkschr. Gesamtakad.* 4:1-236.

———. Forthcoming. Urban archaeology in Egypt. In *Ancient Egypt: Problems of history, sources and methods*, eds. D. O'Connor and D. Redford. Warminster, England: Aris & Phillips, Ltd.

Bietak, Manfred, and Engelmayer, R. 1963. Eine Frühdynastische Abri-Siedlung mit Felsbildern aus Sayala-Nubien. *Denkschr. Akad. Wiss. Österreich. Phil. Hist. Kl.* 82:1-50.

Boessneck, Joachim. 1953. Die Haustiere in Altägypten. *Veröffentl. Zool. Staatssammlung München* 3:1-50.

———. 1960. Zur Gänsehaltung im alten Ägypten. *Wien. Tierärztl. Monatsschr.* (Festschrift Schrieber): 192-206.

Boinet, A. (Bey). 1886. L'accroisement de la population en Égypte.
    Bull. Inst. Egyptien 7:272-305.

———. 1899. *Dictionnaire géographique de l'Égypte.* Cairo: Gov-
    ernment Press. 649 pp.

Borchardt, Ludwig. 1934. Nachträge zu Nilmesser und Nilstandsmar-
    ken. *Abhandl. Akad. Wiss. Berlin Phil. Hist. Kl.*, pp. 194-202.

Boserup, Ester. 1965. *The condition of agricultural growth: The
    economics of agrarian change under population pressure.*
    Chicago: Aldine Pub. Co. 124 pp.

Braidwood, R. J., and Reed, C.A. 1957. The achievement and early
    consequences of food-production: A consideration of the arch-
    eological and natural-historical evidence. *Cold Spring Har-
    bor Symp. Quant. Biol.* 22:19-31.

Breasted, J. H. 1906. *Ancient records of Egypt: IV.* Chicago:
    University of Chicago Press. 520 pp.

Brothwell, D. R., and Chiarelli, B.A., eds. 1973. *Population
    biology of the ancient Egyptians.* London: Academic Press.
    499 pp. + 168 pp.

Brown, R. H. 1887. The Bahr Jusuf: Rough description of its
    present state. *Proc. Roy. Soc. London* 9:614-17.

Brunton, Guy. 1927. *Qau and Badari I*, 44:1-89. London: British
    School of Archaeology in Egypt.

Brunton, Guy, and Caton-Thompson, G. 1928. *The Badarian civili-
    zation*, 46:1-128. London: British School of Archaeology in
    Egypt.

Bruyère, Bernard. 1939. *Rapport sur les fouilles de Deir el Médineh
    (1934-35): III. Le village*, 16:3-78. Cairo: Institut Fran-
    çais d'Archéologie Orientale.

Burleigh, Richard; Switsur, V.R.; and Renfrew, C. 1973. The
    radiocarbon calendar recalibrated too? *Antiquity* 47:309-17.

Butzer, K. W. 1958. Das ökologische Problem der neolithischen
    Felsbilder der östlichen Sahara. *Abhandl. Akad. Wiss. Mainz Lit.
    Math.-Naturw. Kl.*, no. 1, pp. 20-49.

———. 1959a. Contributions to the Pleistocene geology of the Nile
    Valley. *Erdkunde* 13:46-67.

———. 1959b. Die Naturlandschaft Ägyptens während der Vorgeschichte
    und der Dynastischen Zeit. *Abhandl. Akad. Wiss. Mainz Lit. Math.-
    Naturw. Kl.*, no. 2, pp. 1-80.

———. 1959c. Environment and human ecology in Egypt during Pre-
    dynastic and Early Dynastic times. *Bull. Soc. Géograph.
    Egypte* 32:43-87.

———. 1960a. Remarks on the geography of settlement in the Nile Valley during Hellenistic times. *Bull. Soc. Géograph. Egypte* 33:5-36.

———. 1960b. Archeology and geology in ancient Egypt. *Science* 132:1617-24.

———. 1961. Archäologische Fundstellen Ober- und Mittelägyptens in ihrer geologischen Landschaft. *Mitt. Deut. Archäol. Inst. Abteilung Kairo* 17:54-68.

———. 1971a. *Environment and archeology: An ecological approach to prehistory*. Chicago: Aldine Pub. Co. 705 pp.

———. 1971b. *Recent history of an Ethiopian Delta: The Omo Delta and the level of Lake Rudolf*. Research Papers, vol. 136, pp. 1-184. Chicago: University of Chicago, Department of Geography.

———. 1973. Bahr Jussuf. *Lex. Ägyptol.* 1:602.

———. 1974. Delta. *Lex. Ägyptol.* 1:1043-52.

———. 1975a. Patterns of environmental change in the Near East during late Pleistocene and early Holocene times. In *Problems in prehistory: North Africa and the Levant*, eds. F. Wendorf and A. E. Marks, pp. 389-410. Dallas: Southern Methodist University Press.

———. 1975b. Pleistocene littoral sedimentary cycles of the Mediterranean Basin: A Mallorquin view. In *After the Australopithecines*, eds. K. W. Butzer and G. L. Isaac, pp. 25-71. The Hague: Mouton.

Butzer, K. W.; Brown, F. H.; and Thurber, D. L. 1969. Horizontal sediments of the lower Omo Valley: The Kibish Formation. *Quarternaria* 11:31-46.

Butzer, K. W., and Hansen, C. L. 1968. *Desert and river in Nubia: Geomorphology and prehistoric environments at the Aswan Reservoir*. Madison: University of Wisconsin Press. 562 pp.

———. 1972. Late Pleistocene stratigraphy of the Kom Ombo plain, Upper Egypt: A comparison with other recent studies near Esna-Edfu. *Bull. Assoc. Sénégalaise Etude Quaternaire de l'Ouest Afr.*, no. 3536, pp. 5-14.

Butzer, K. W.; Isaac, G. L.; Richardson, J. L.; and Washbourn-Kamau, C. K. 1972. Radiocarbon dating of East African lake levels. *Science* 175:1069-76.

Cadell, Hélène. 1970. Le vocabulaire de l'agriculture d'après les papyrus grecs d'Egypte: Problèmes et voies de recherche. *Am. Stud. Papyrol.* 7:69-76.

Camps, Gabriel. 1969. Amekni: Néolithique ancien du Hoggar.
    Mem. Cent. Recherches Anthropol. Préhist. Ethnograph. 10:1-230.
———. 1975. The prehistoric cultures of North Africa: Radiocarbon
    chronology. In *The Pleistocene prehistory of the southern
    and eastern Mediterranean Basin,* eds. F. Wendorf and A. E.
    Marks, pp. 181-92. Dallas: Southern Methodist University
    Press.
Camps, Gabriel; Délibrias, G; and Thommeret, J. 1973. Chrono-
    logie absolue des civilisations préhistoriques du nord de
    l'Afrique d'après le radiocarbone. *Libyca* 21:65-89.
Carneiro, R. L. 1972. From autonomous villages to the state:
    A numerical estimation. In *Population growth: Anthropolo-
    gical implications,* ed. B. Spooner, pp. 64-77. Cambridge:
    M.I.T. Press.
Carr, C. J. Forthcoming. *The Dasenitch of southwest Ethiopia:
    A system of societal/environmental change.* Research Papers.
    Chicago: University of Chicago, Department of Geography.
Caton-Thompson, Gertrude. 1946. The Levalloisian industries of
    Egypt. *Proc. Prehist. Soc.* 12:57-120.
———. 1952. *The Kharga Oasis in prehistory.* London: Athlone
    Press. 213 pp.
Caton-Thompson, Gertrude, and Gardner, E. W. 1929. Recent work
    on the problem of Lake Moeris. *Geograph. J.* 73:20-60.
———. 1932. The prehistoric geography of the Kharga Oasis. *Geo-
    graph. J.* 80:369-409.
———. 1934. *The Desert Fayum.* 2 vols. London: Royal Anthropo-
    logical Society.
Caton-Thompson, Gertrude; Gardner, E.W.; and Huzayyin, S.A. 1937.
    Lake Moeris: Re-investigations and some comments. *Bull.
    Inst. Egypte* 19:243-303.
Černý, Jaroslav. 1933. Fluctuations in grain prices during the
    20th Egyptian Dynasty. *Arch. Orientalni* 6:173-78.
———. 1939. Late Ramesside letters. *Bibliotheca Aegyptiaca*
    9:1-20.
———. 1954. Prices and wages in Egypt in the Ramesside period.
    Cahiers Hist. Univ. 1:903-21.
———. 1955. Some Coptic etymologies. In *Grapow Festschrift,* ed.
    O. Firchow, pp. 30-37. Berlin: Deutsche Akademie der Wis-
    senschaften, Institut für Orientforschung.
———. 1965. Egypt from the death of Ramesses III to the end of
    the 21st Dynasty. In *Cambridge Ancient History,* rev. ed.,

2, pt. 2:1-60.

Červiček, Pavel. 1973. Datierung der nordafrikanischen Felsbilder durch die Patina. *Ipek* 23:82-87.

Childe, V. G. 1929. *The most ancient East*. London: Routledge and Kegan Paul, Ltd. 258 pp.

Christaller, Walter. 1966. *Central places in southern Germany*. Englewood Cliffs, New Jersey: Prentice-Hall. 230 pp.

Churcher, C. S. 1972. Late Pleistocene vertebrates from archeological sites in the Plain of Kom Ombo, Upper Egypt. *Life Sci. Contr. Roy. Ont. Mus.* 82:1-172.

Clark, J. D. 1971. A re-examination of the evidence for agricultural origins in the Nile Valley. *Proc. Prehist. Soc.* 37:34-79.

Conrad, Georges. 1969. *L'évolution continentale post-hercynienne du Sahara algérien*. Paris: Centre Nationale des Recherches Scientifiques. 527 pp.

Cowgill, G. L. 1974. Quantitative studies of urbanization at Teotihuacán. In *Mesoamerican archaeology: New approaches*, ed. N. Hammond, pp. 363-96. London: Duckworth & Co., Ltd.

---. 1975a. Population pressure as a non-explanation. In *Population studies in archaeology and biological anthropology*, ed. Alan Swedlund. Memoirs, vol. 30, pp. 127-33. Washington, D.C.: Society for American Archaeology.

---. 1975b. On causes and consequences of ancient and modern population changes. *Am. Anthropol.* 78:505-25.

Crawford, D. J. 1971. *Kerkeosiris: An Egyptian village in the Ptolemaic period*. Cambridge: Cambridge University Press. 238 pp.

Crouchley, A. E. 1938. *Economic development of modern Egypt*. London: Longman Group Ltd. 286 pp.

Curray, J. R., et al. 1970. Late Quaternary sea-level studies in Micronesia. *Bull. Geol. Soc. Am.* 81:1865-80.

Daniel, Glyn. 1967. *The origins and growth of archaeology*. Harmondsworth, England: Penguin Books Ltd. 304 pp.

Davies, Norman de G. 1903. *The rock tombs of El-Amarna*. Vol. 1. London: Egypt Exploration Fund. 55 pp.

---. 1929. The graphic work of the expedition. *Bull. Metropolitan Mus. Art* 24 (November, Sect. II). 49 pp.

---. 1933. *The tomb of Nefer-Hotep at Thebes*. Vol. 1. Publication 9. New York: Metropolitan Museum of Art Egyptian Expedition. 81 pp.

Derricourt, R. M. 1971. Radiocarbon chronology for Egypt and North Africa. *J. Near East. Stud.* 30:271-92.

Derry, D. E. 1956. The dynastic race in Egypt. *J. Egypt. Arch-aeol.* 42:80-85.

Desroches-Noblecourt, Christiane. 1950. Un petit monument commé-moratif du roi athlète. *Rev. Egyptol.* 7:37-46.

Dixon, D. M. 1969. A note on cereals in ancient Egypt. In *The domestication and exploitation of plants and animals,* eds. P. J. Ucko and G. W. Dimbleby, pp. 131-42. Chicago: Aldine Pub. Co.

Donadoni, Sergio. Forthcoming. Outstanding problems of Graeco-Roman archaeology. In *Ancient Egypt: Problems of history, sources and methods,* eds. D. O'Connor and D. Redford. War-minster, England: Aris & Phillips, Ltd.

Downing, T. E., and Gibson, McG., eds. 1974. *Irrigation's im-pact on society.* Anthropological Papers, vol. 25, pp. 1-181. Tucson: University of Arizona.

Drioton, Étienne. 1947. Notes diverses: Deux scarabées commémo-ratifs d'Amenophis III. *Ann. Serv. Antiq. Egypte* 45:85-92.

Dunham, Dows. 1938. The biographical inscriptions of Nebhebu in Boston and Cairo. *J. Egypt. Archaeol.* 24:1-8.

Edel, Elmar. 1961-64. Zu den Inschriften auf den Jahreszeiten-reliefs der "Weltkammer" aus dem Sonnenheiligtum des Niuserre. *Nach. Akad. Wiss. Göttingen Phil. Hist. Kl.,* no. 8 (1961), pp. 199-255; nos. 4-5 (1963), pp. 87-217.

Edwards, I.E.S.. 1961. *The pyramids of Egypt.* New York: Viking Press Inc. 240 pp.

---. 1971. The Early Dynastic period in Egypt. In *Cambridge Ancient History,* rev. ed., 1, 2:1-70.

Emery, K. O., and Bentor, Y. K. 1960. The continental shelf of Israel. *Bull. Israel Geol. Survey* 26:25-38.

Emery, W. B. 1961. *Archaic Egypt.* Harmondsworth, England: Penguin Books, Ltd. 261 pp.

Epstein, H. 1971. *The origin of the domestic animals of Africa.* New York: Africana Pub. Co. 2 vols. 573 + 719 pp.

Erhart, M. H., Pias, J., and Leneuf, G. 1954. *Étude pédologique de bassin alluvionnaire du Logone-Chari.* Paris: Office des Recherches Scientifiques et Techniques d'Outre-Mer. 234 pp.

Erman, Adolf. 1885. *Ägypten und ägyptisches Leben im Altertum.* Tübingen, Germany: (Verlag) Laupp. 745 pp.

Fairman, H. W. 1949. Town planning in Pharaonic Egypt. *Town Planning Rev.* 20:33-51.

Fairservis, W. A. 1972. Preliminary report on the first two seasons at Hierakonpolis. *J. Am. Res. Cent. Egypt* 9:7-27, 67-99.

Fakhry, Ahmed. 1973a. *The oases of Egypt.* Vol. 1. *Siwa Oasis.* Cairo: American University in Cairo Press. 214 pp.

---. 1973b. Bahrija. *Lex. Ägyptol.* 1:601-4.

---. 1974a. Charga. *Lex. Ägyptol.* 1:907-10.

---. 1974b. Dachel. *Lex. Ägyptol.* 1:976-79.

Faure, Hughes. 1966. Evolution des grands lacs sahariens à l'Holocène. *Quaternaria* 8:167-75.

Fecht, Gerhard. 1972. Der Vorwurf an Gott in den "Mahnworten des Ipu-wer." *Abhandl. Heidelberg Akad. Wiss. Phil. Hist. Kl.* 1:1-240.

Fischer, H. G. 1964. Inscriptions from the Coptite nome. *Analecta Orientalia* 40:1-142.

---. 1969. *Dendera in the third millennium B.C., down to the Theban Dominion.* Locust Valley, N. Y.: J. J. Augustin. 246 pp.

---. Forthcoming. Archaeological aspects of epigraphy and palaeography. In *Ancient Egypt: Problems of history, sources and methods*, eds. D. O'Connor and D. Redford. Warminster, England: Aris & Phillips, Ltd.

Fourtau, René. 1915. Contribution à l'étude des dépôts nilotiques. *Mem. Inst. Egypte* 8:57-94.

Frankfort, Henri. 1948. *Kingship and the gods: A study of ancient Near Eastern religion as the integration of society and nature.* Chicago: University of Chicago Press. 444 pp.

---. 1951. *The birth of civilization in the Near East.* Bloomington: Indiana University Press. 116 pp. (2nd ed., 1956, 142 pp.)

Gaillard, Claude. 1923. Recherches sur les poissons représentés dans quelques tombeaux égyptiens de l'Ancien Empire. *Mem. Inst. Fr. Archéol. Orientale* 51:1-136.

Gamer-Wallert, I. 1970. Fische und Fischkulte im alten Ägypten. *Ägyptol. Abhandl.* 21:1-100.

Gardiner, A. H. 1944. Horus the Behdetite. *J. Egypt. Archaeol.* 30:23-60.

---. 1947. *Ancient Egyptian Onomastica.* 2 vols. Oxford: Oxford University Press. 68+215*+324* pp.

---. 1948. *The Wilbour Papyrus.* Vol. 2. *Commentary.* Oxford: Oxford University Press. 216 pp.

Gasse, Françoise; Fontes, J.C.; Rognon, P. 1974. Variations hydrologiques et extension des lacs holocènes du Désert Danakil.

Palaeogeograph. Palaeoclimatol. Palaeoecol. 15:109-48.

Gauthier, Henri. 1925-31. *Dictionnaire des noms géographiques, contenus dans les textes hieroglyphiques, I-VII.* Cairo: Institut Français d'Archéologie Orientale.

---. 1935. Les noms d'Egypte depuis Hérodote jusqu'à la conquête arabe. *Mem. Inst. Egypte* 25:1-219.

Ghalioungui, Paul. 1969. Parasitic disease in Ancient Egypt. *Bull. Inst. Egypte* 48-49:13-26.

Gibson, McGuire. 1974. Violation of fallow and engineered disaster in Mesopotamian civilization. In *Irrigation's impact on society*, eds. T. E. Downing and McG. Gibson. Anthropological Papers, vol. 25, pp. 7-20. Tucson: University of Arizona.

Giles, F. J. 1970. *Ikhnaton: Legend and history.* London: Hutchinson Publishing Group Ltd. 255 pp.

Goyon, Georges. 1971. Les ports des pyramides et le grand canal de Memphis. *Rev. Egyptol.* 23:137-53.

Graefe, Erhart. 1973. Einige Bemerkungen zur Angabe der *st3t-* Grösse auf der weissen Kapelle Sesostris I. *J. Egypt. Arch.* 59:72-76.

Greenberg, J. H. 1955. *Studies in African linguistic classification.* New Haven: Compass Publications. 116 pp.

Greene, D. L. 1972. Dental anthropology of early Egypt and Nubia. *J. Human Evol.* 1:315-24.

Greene, D. L., and Armelagos, G. 1972. *The Wadi Halfa Mesolithic population.* Research Report, vol. 11, pp. 1-144. Amherst: Department of Anthropology, University of Massachusetts.

Guichard, Jean, and Guichard, G. 1965. The Early and Middle Palaeolithic of Nubia: A preliminary report. In *Contributions to the prehistory of Nubia*, ed. F. Wendorf, pp. 57-116. Dallas: Southern Methodist University Press.

Habachi, L. 1974. A high inundation mark in the temple of Amenre at Karnak in the 13th Dynasty. *Stud. Altägypt. Kultur* 1:207-14.

Hafemann, Dieter. 1960. Die Frage des eustatischen Meeresspiegel-anstiegs in historischer Zeit. *Abhandl. Deut. Geographentag Berlin*, pp. 218-31.

Haggett, Peter. 1966. *Locational analysis in human geography.* New York: St. Martin's Press, Inc. 339 pp.

Halawani, A., and Shawarby, A. A. 1957. Malaria in Egypt. *J. Egypt. Med. Assoc.* 40:753-92.

Hamdan, G. 1961. Evolution of irrigation agriculture in Egypt. *Arid Zone Research* 17:119-42.

Hammond, Norman. 1974. *Mesoamerican archeology: New approaches.* London: Duckworth & Co., Ltd.

Harlan, J. R., and Zohary, D. 1966. Distribution of wild wheats and barley. *Science* 153: 1074-80.

Harrison, J. C. 1955. An interpretation of gravity anomalies in the Eastern Mediterranean. *Phil. Trans. Roy. Soc. (London)* A-248:283-325.

Hartmann, Fernande. 1923. *L'agriculture dans l'ancienne Egypte.* Paris: Lib.-Imp. Réunis. 332 pp.

Hassan, F. A. 1972. Population dynamics and the beginnings of domestication in the Nile Valley. Paper read at the seventy-first meeting of the American Anthropological Association, Toronto. Mimeographed.

---. 1974. Population growth and cultural evolution. *Rev. Anthropol.* 1:205-12.

---. 1975. *The archaeology of the Dishna Plain,* paper 59, pp. 1-174. Cairo: Geological Survey of Egypt.

---. Forthcoming. Determinants of the size, density, and growth rate of hunting-gathering populations. In *Population, adaptation, and evolution,* ed. S. Polgar. The Hague: Mouton.

Hayes, W. C. 1951. Inscriptions from the palace of Amenophis III. *J. Near East. Stud.* 10:82-104.

---. 1964. Most ancient Egypt. *J. Near East. Stud.* 23:73-114, 145-92, 217-74.

Heinzelin, Jean de. 1964. Le sous-sol du temple d'Aksha. *Kush* 12:102-10.

Helbaek, Hans. 1959. Domestication of food plants in the Old World. *Science* 130:365-73.

Helck, Wolfgang. 1958. Zur Verwaltung des mittleren und neuen Reiches. In *Probleme der Ägyptologie.* Vol. 3. Leiden: E. J. Brill. 550 pp.

---. 1960-64. Materialien zur Wirtschaftsgeschichte des Neuen Reiches. *Abhandl. Akad. Wiss. Mainz Lit. Geistes Sozialwiss. Kl.,* nos. 10 and 11 (1960); nos. 2 and 3 (1963); no. 4 (1964). 944 pp.

---. 1974a. Die altägyptischen Gaue. *Beih. Tübinger Atlas Vorderen Orients* B-5:1-216.

---. 1974b. Bürgermeister. *Lex. Ägyptol.* 1:875-80.

Herold, J. C.   1962. *Bonaparte in Egypt*. London: Hamish
    Hamilton, Ltd. 424 pp.
Hilzheimer, Max. 1926. Säugetierkunde und Archäologie. *Z. Saüge-
    tierkunde* 1:140-69.
---. 1930. Die ältesten Beziehungen zwischen Asien und Afrika,
    nachgewiesen an den Haustieren. *Afrika* 3:472-83.
Hobler, P. M., and Hester, J. J. 1969. Prehistory and environment
    in the Libyan Desert. *S. Afr. Archaeol. Bull.* 33:120-30.
Hoffman, Michael. 1972. Occupational features at the Kom el-Ahmar:
    Test excavations at locality 14. *J. Am. Res. Cent. Egypt*
    9:35-66.
Holz, R. K. 1969. Man-made landforms in the Nile Delta. *Geograph.
    Rev.* 59:253-69.
Hughes, G. R. 1952. Saite Demotic leases. *Chicago Stud. Ancient
    Oriental Civ.* 28:1-111.
Hurst, H. E., and Phillips, P. 1931-36. *The Nile Basin*. Vols. 1
    and 3. Cairo: Physical Department, Government Press. 144 +
    715 pp.
Huzayyin, S. A. 1941. The place of Egypt in prehistory. *Mem. Inst.
    Egypte* 43:1-474.
Jacotin, E. 1826. *Atlas géographique: Description de l'Égypte*.
    Paris: Panckoucke. 48 map plates (1:100,000).
Jacquet-Gordon, Helen. 1962. *Les noms des domaines funéraires sous
    l'ancien ampire égyptien*, 34:1-505. Cairo: Bibliothéque
    d'Etude, Institut Francais d'Archéologie Orientale.
James, T. G. H. 1962. *The Hekanakhte papers and other early Middle
    Kingdom documents*. Publication 19. New York: Metropolitan
    Museum of Art Egyptian Expedition. 146 pp.
---. 1973. Egypt from the expulsion of the Hyksos to Amenophis I.
    In *Cambridge Ancient History*, rev. ed., 2, pt. 1:289-312.
Janssen, J. J. 1975a. *Commodity prices from the Ramessid period:
    An economic study of the village of necropolis workmen at
    Thebes*. Leiden: E. J. Brill. 601 pp.
---. 1975b. Prolegomena to the study of Egypt's economic history
    during the New Kingdom. *Stud. Altägypt. Kultur* 3:127-85.
Jenny, Hans. 1962. Model of a rising nitrogen profile in Nile
    Valley alluvium. *Proc. Soil Sci. Soc. Am.* 26:588-91.
Johnson, A. C., and West, L. C. 1949. *Byzantine Egypt: Economic
    studies*. Princeton, N.J.: Princeton University Press. 344 pp.
Johnson, G. A. 1975. Locational analysis and the investigation of
    Uruk local exchange systems. In *Ancient civilization and*

trade, eds. J. A. Sabloff and C. C. Lamberg-Karlovsky, pp. 285-339. Albuquerque: University of New Mexico Press.

Kaiser, Werner. 1961. Bericht über eine archäologisch-geologische Felduntersuchung in Ober- und Mittelägypten. *Mitt. Deut. Archäol. Inst. Abteilung Kairo* 17:1-53.

---. 1964. Einige Bemerkungen zur ägyptischen Frühzeit. *Z. Ägypt. Sprache* 91:86-125.

---. 1974. *Studien zur Vergeschichte Ägyptens: I. Die Nagada-kultur.* Glückstadt, Germany: Augustin.

Kaiser, Werner; Grossmann, P.; Haeny, G.; and Jaritz, H. 1974. Stadt und Tempel von Elephantine. *Mitt. Deut. Archäol. Inst. Abteilung Kairo* 30:65-90.

Kamal, Hassan. 1967. *Dictionary of Pharaonic medicine.* Cairo: National Publication House. 509 pp.

Kees, Hermann. 1961. *Ancient Egypt: A cultural topography,* ed. T.G.H. James. Chicago: University of Chicago Press. 392 pp.

Keimer, Ludwig. 1938. Remarques sur quelques répresentations de béliers. *Ann. Serv. Antiq. Egypte* 38:297-332.

Kemp, B. J. 1972a. Temple and town in ancient Egypt. In *Man, settlement and urbanism,* eds. P. J. Ucko, R. Tringham, and G. W. Dimbleby, pp. 657-80. London: Duckworth & Co., Ltd.

---. 1972b. Fortified towns in Nubia. In *Man, settlement and urbanism,* eds. P. J. Ucko, R. Tringham, and G. W. Dimbleby, pp. 651-56. London: Duckworth & Co., Ltd.

---. In press. A note on stratigraphy at Memphis. *J. Am. Res. Cent. Egypt.*

Kemp, B. J., and O'Connor, D. 1974. An ancient Nile harbour: University Museum excavations at the "Birket Habu." *Intern. J. Naut. Archaeol. Underwater Explor.* 3:101-36.

Kholief, M. M.; Hilmy, E.; and Shahat, A. 1969. Geological and mineralogical studies of some sand deposits in the Nile Delta, U. A. R. *J. Sediment. Petrol.* 39:1520-29.

Kitchen, K. A. 1973. *The Third Intermediate Period in Egypt (1100-650 B.C.).* Warminster, England: Aris & Phillips, Ltd. 525 pp.

Klebs, Luise. 1915. *Die Reliefs des Alten Reiches.* Heidelberg: Winters. 150 pp.

Kobishchanov, I. M. 1966. *Aksum.* Moscow: Akademiya Nauk SSSR. 286 pp.

Kraeling, C. H., and Adams, R. M., eds. 1960. *City invincible: An Oriental Institute Symposium.* Chicago: University of Chicago Press. 448 pp.

Lacau, Pierre, and Chevrier, H., 1956. *Une chapelle de Sesostris I à Karnak.* Cairo: Service des Antiquités de l'Égypte. 284 pp.

Lane, E. W. 1860. *The manners and customs of the modern Egyptians.* 2nd ed. London: Dent & Sons, Ltd. 630 pp.

Larsen, C. E. 1975. The Mesopotamian delta region: A reconsideration of Lees and Falcon. *J. Am. Oriental Soc.* 95:43-57.

Larsen, Hjalmar. 1957. On a detail of the Nagada plant. *Ann. Serv. Antiq. Egypte* 54:239-44.

Leopold, L. B.; Wolman, M. G.; and Miller, J. P., 1964. *Fluvial processes in geomorphology.* San Francisco: W.H. Freeman & Co. 522 pp.

Lind, A. O. 1969. *Coastal landforms of Cat Island, Bahamas: A study of Holocene accretionary topography and sea-level change.* Research Papers, vol. 122, pp. 1-156. Chicago: University of Chicago, Department of Geography.

Loret, Victor. 1892. *La flore pharaonique d'après les documents hieroglyphiques et les spécimens découverts dans les tombes.* Paris: E. Leroux. 145 pp.

Lozach, J. 1935. *Le Delta du Nil: Étude de géographie humaine.* Cairo: Société de Géographie d'Egypte. 303 pp.

Lucas, Alfred, and Harris, J. R. 1962. *Ancient Egyptian materials and industries.* London: Arnold, Ltd. 523 pp.

Lukermann, F. E. 1972. Settlement and circulation: Pattern and systems. In *The Minnesota Messenia Expedition: Reconstructing a Bronze Age regional environment,* eds. W. A. McDonald and G. R. Rapp, pp. 148-70. Minneapolis: University of Minnesota Press.

Maitre, J. P. 1971. Contribution à la préhistoire de l'Ahaggar: I. Téfédest centrale. *Mem. Cent. Recherches Anthropol. Prehist. Ethnograph.* 17:1-225.

McBurney, C. B. M. 1960. *The Stone Age of northern Africa.* Harmondsworth, England: Penguin Books, Ltd. 288 pp.

McHugh, W. P. 1975. Some archaeological results of the Bagnold-Mond Expedition to the Gilf Kebir and Gebel Uweinat, southern Libyan Desert. *J. Near East. Stud.* 34:31-62.

Mikesell, M. W. 1955. Notes on the dispersal of the dromedary. *Southwestern J. Anthropol.* 11:231-45.

Misdorp, R., and Sestini, G. Forthcoming. Topography of the
    continental shelf of the Nile Delta. In *Proceedings of
    Seminar on Nile Delta Sedimentology*, 25-29 October 1975,
    Alexandria: UNESCO.

Montet, Pierre. 1954. Les boeufs égyptiens. *Kemi* 13:42-58.

---. 1957-61. *Géographie de l'Égypte ancienne*. Vol. 1. *La Basse
    Egypte*. Vol. 2. *La Haute Egypte*. Paris: Klincksieck.
    224+237 pp.

Mori, Fabrizio. 1965. *Tadrart Acacus: Arte rupestre ·e culture
    del Sahara preistorico*. Turin: Einaudi. 257 pp.

Murray, G. W. 1951. The Egyptian climate: An historical outline.
    Geograph. J. 117:422-34.

---. 1952. Early camels in Egypt. *Bull. Inst. Désert* 2:105-6.

---. 1955. Water from the desert: Some ancient Egyptian achieve-
    ments. *Geograph. J.* 121:171-87.

Naville, Edouard. 1906. *Deir el-Bahari*. Vol. 5, pl. 119-50.
    London: Egypt Exploration Society.

Neely, J. A. 1974. Sassanian and early Islamic water-control
    and irrigation systems on the Deh Luran Plain, Iran. In
    Irrigation's impact on society, eds. T. E. Downing and McG.
    Gibson, Anthropological Papers, vol. 25, pp. 21-42. Tucson:
    University of Arizona.

Newberry, P. E. 1925. Egypt as a field for anthropological
    research. In *Annual Report, Smithsonian Institution, 1924*,
    pp. 435-59. Washington, D.C.: Smithsonian Institution.

Niemeier, Georg. 1972. *Siedlungsgeographie*. 3rd ed. Braun-
    schweig, Germany: Westermann. 181 pp.

Niemeier, Wolfgang. 1936. *Ägypten zur Zeit der Mamluken: Eine
    kultur-landeskundliche Skizze*. Berlin: Reimer. 196 pp.

Nims, C. F. 1955. Places about Thebes. *J. Near East. Stud.*
    14:110-21.

O'Connor, David. 1972a. The geography of settlement in ancient
    Egypt. In *Man, settlement and urbanism*, eds. P. J. Ucko, R.
    Tringham, and G. W. Dimbleby, pp. 681-98. London: Duckworth
    & Co., Ltd.

---. 1972b. A regional population in Egypt to circa 600 B.C.
    In *Population growth: Anthropological implications*, ed.
    B. Spooner, pp. 78-100. Cambridge: M.I.T. Press.

---. 1974. Political systems and archaeological data in Egypt
    2600-1780 B.C. *World Archaeol.* 6:15-38.

O'Connor, David, and Redford, D. Forthcoming. *Ancient Egypt:*
    Problems of history, sources and methods, eds. D. O'Connor
    and D. Redford, Warminster, England: Aris & Phillips, Ltd.
Otto, Eberhard. 1952. Topographie des Thebanischen Gaues.
    Untersuchungen Geschichte Altertumskunde Ägyptens 16:1-123.
Passarge, Siegfried. 1940. Die Urlandschaft Ägyptens und die
    Lokalisierung der Wiege der altägyptischen Kultur. *Nova*
    Acta Leopoldina 9:77-152.
Petrie, W. M. F. 1891. *Illahun, Kahun and Gurob.* Reprint 1974.
    Warminster, England: Aris & Phillips, Ltd. 59 pp.
Phillips, J. L., and Butzer, K. W. 1975. A "Silsilian" occu-
    pation site (GS-2B-II) of the Kom Ombo Plain, Upper Egypt:
    Geology, archeology and paleo-ecology. *Quaternaria* 17 (1973):
    1-45.
Polgar, Steven. 1972. Population history and population policies
    from an anthropological perspective. *Curr. Anthropol.* 13:
    203-11.
---., ed. Forthcoming. *Population, adaptation, and evolution.*
    The Hague: Mouton.
Popper, William. 1951. The Cairo Nilometer: Studies in Ibn Taghru
    Birdi's Chronicles of Egypt. *Univ. Calif. (Berkeley) Publ.*
    Sem. Philol. 12:1-269.
Porter, Bertha, and Moss, R. J. L. 1927-51. *Topographical bib-*
    liography of ancient Egyptian hieroglyphic texts, reliefs and
    paintings: I. Theban necropolis (1927) 212 pp.; *II. The-*
    ban temples (1929) 203 pp.; *III. Memphis* (1931) 254 pp.;
    IV. Lower and Middle Egypt (1934) 294 pp.; *V. Upper Egypt:*
    Sites (1937) 292 pp.; *VI. Upper Egypt: Chief temples* (1939)
    264 pp.; *VII. Nubia, the desert, and outside Egypt* (1951)
    453 pp. Oxford: Oxford University Press.
Pouquet, Jean. 1969. Géomorphologie et ére spatiale. *Z. Geomor-*
    phol. 13:414-71.
Prominska, Elzbieta. 1972. Investigations on the population of
    Muslim Alexandria. *Trav. Cent. Archéol. Med. Acad. Polonaise*
    Sci. (Warsaw) 12:1-124.
Quibell, J. E. 1900. *Hierakonpolis: Part 1.* Memoir 4. London:
    B. Quaritch for Egyptian Research Account. 49 pl.
Ralph, E. K.; Michael, H. N.; and Han, M. C. 1973. Radiocarbon
    dates and reality. *MASCA Newsl.* 9:1-20.

Redford, D.   Forthcoming.   The historiography of ancient Egypt.
    In *Ancient Egypt: Problems of history, sources and methods*,
    eds. D. O'Connor and D. Redford.   Warminster, England: Aris
    & Phillips, Ltd.

Reed, C. A.   1969.   The pattern of animal domestication in the
    prehistoric Near East.   In *The domestication and exploitation
    of animals*, eds. P. J. Ucko and G. W. Dimbleby, pp. 361-80.
    Chicago: Aldine Pub. Co.

Renfrew, Colin.   1972.   Patterns of population growth in the pre-
    historic Aegean.   In *Man, settlement and urbanism*, eds. P. J.
    Ucko, R. Tringham, and G. W. Dimbleby, pp. 383-400.   London:
    Duckworth & Co., Ltd.

Russell, J. C.   1966.   The population of medieval Egypt.   *J. Am.
    Res. Cent. Egypt* 5:69-82.

Saad, S. I., and Sami, S.   1967.   Studies of pollen and spores con-
    tent of Nile Delta deposits (Berenbal region).   *Pollen
    Spores* 9:467-503.

Said, R.; Albritton, C. C.; Wendorf, F.; Schild, R.; and Kobusie-
    wicz, M.   1972.   A preliminary report on the Holocene geology
    and archaeology of the northern Fayum desert.   Playa Lake
    Symposium, Texas Technological University, Lubbock, Texas.
    ICALS Publ. 4:41-61.

Said, Rushdi, and Yousri, F.   1968.   Origin and Pleistocene his-
    tory of River Nile near Cairo, Egypt.   *Bull. Inst. Egypte*
    45(1963/64):1-30.

Salmon, Georges.   1901.   Répertoire géographique de la province
    de Fayyoum d'après le Kitab Tarikh al-Fayyoum d'An-Naboulsi.
    Bull. Inst. Fr. Archéol. Orientale 1:29-77.

Sanders, W. T., and Price, B. J.   1968.   *Mesoamerica: The evolu-
    tion of a civilization*.   New York: Random House, Inc.   264 pp.

Sandford, K. S.   1934.   Paleolithic man and the Nile Valley in
    Middle and Upper Egypt.   *Publ. Univ. Chicago Oriental Inst.*
    8:1-131.

Sandford, K. S., and Arkell, W. J.   1929.   Paleolithic man and the
    Nile-Faiyum divide.   *Publ. Univ. Chicago Oriental Inst.* 10:
    1-77.

———.   1939.   Paleolithic man and the Nile Valley in Lower Egypt.
    Publ. Univ. Chicago Oriental Inst. 46:1-105.

Sauneron, Serge.   1964.   Villes et légendes d'Egypte.   *Bull. Inst.
    Fr. Archéol. Orientale* 62:33-57.

---. Forthcoming. Topographie et toponomie de l'Egypte ancienne.
In *Ancient Egypt: Problems of history, sources and methods*,
eds. D. O'Connor and D. Redford. Warminster, England: Aris
& Phillips, Ltd.

Säve-Söderbergh, Törgny. 1964. Preliminary report of the Scan-
dinavian Joint Expedition: Archeological investigations
between Faras and Gemai, 1962-1963. *Kush* 12:19-39.

---. Forthcoming. Aspects of ancient Egyptian relations with
Nubia and the Sudan. In *Ancient Egypt: Problems of his-
tory, sources and methods*, eds. D. O'Connor and D. Redford.
Warminster, England: Aris & Phillips, Ltd.

Schenkel, Wolfgang. 1962. Frühmittelägyptische Studien. *Bonn.
Orient. Stud.* 13:1-160.

---. 1973. Be- und Entwässerung. *Lex. Ägyptol.* 1:775-82.

---. 1974. Die Einfuhrüng der künstlichen Feldbewässerung im alten Ägypten. *Gött. Misc.: Beitr. ägyptol. Disk.*, no. 11, pp.
41-46.

Schild, Romuald; Chmielewska, M.; and Wieckowska, H. 1968. The
Arkinian and Shamarkian industries. In *The prehistory of
Nubia*, ed. F. Wendorf, pp. 651-767. Dallas: Southern
Methodist University Press.

Schild, Romuald, and Wendorf, F. 1975. New explorations in the
Egyptian Sahara. In *Problems in prehistory: North Africa
and the Levant*, eds. Fred Wendorf and A. E. Marks, pp. 65-112.
Dallas: Southern Methodist University Press.

Schlott, Adelheid. 1969. Die Ausmasse Ägyptens nach altägyptischen Texten, Dissertation, Darmstadt.

---. 1973. Altägyptische Texte über die Ausmasse Ägyptens.
Mitt. Deut. Archaeol. Inst. Abteilung Kairo 72:109-13.

Schnebel, Michael. 1925. Die Landwirtschaft im hellenistischen
Ägypten: I. *Münch. Beitr. Papyrusforsch. Antiken Rechtsgesch.*
7:1-379.

Servant, Michel; Servant, S.; and Délibrias, G. 1969. Chronologie du Quaternaire récent des basses régions du Tchad. *Compt.
Rend. Acad. Sci. (Paris)* D-269:1603-6.

Sestini, Giuliano. Forthcoming. Geomorphology of the Nile Delta.
In *Proceedings of Seminar on Nile Delta Sedimentology*, 25-29
October 1975. Alexandria: UNESCO.

Sethe, Kurt. 1906. *Urkunden der 18. Dynastie (IV. Abteilung)*.
Leipzig: Hinrich.

---. 1933. *Urkunden des Alten Reiches (I. Abteilung)*. Leipzig:
    Hinrich.

Shafei, Ali. 1940. Fayoum irrigation as described by Nabulsi.
    Bull. Soc. Géograph. Egypte 20:283-327.

---. 1952. Lake Mareotis: Its past history and its future deve-
    lopment. *Bull. Inst. Désert* 2:71-101.

Shiner, J. L. 1968. The cataract tradition. In *The prehistory
    of Nubia*, ed. F. Wendorf, pp. 535-629. Dallas: Southern
    Methodist University Press.

Shousha, A. T. 1948. Species eradication: The eradication of
    Anopheles gambiae from Upper Egypt. *Bull. WHO* 1:309-52.

Simons, Peter. 1968. Die Entwicklung des Anbaus und die Ver-
    breitung der Nutzpflanzen in der ägyptischen Nilstromoase von
    1800 bis zur Gegenwart. *Kölner Geograph. Arb.* 20:1-217.

Simpson, W. K. 1963. Studies in the 12th Egyptian Dynasty: The
    residence of Itj-Towy. *J. Am. Res. Cent. Egypt* 2:53-58.

Smith, H. S. 1969. Animal domestication and animal cult in Dynas-
    tic Egypt. In *The domestication and exploitation of plants
    and animals*, eds. P. J. Ucko and G. W . Dimbleby, pp. 307-
    14. Chicago: Aldine Pub. Co.

---. 1972. Society and settlement in ancient Egypt. In *Man,
    settlement and urbanism*, eds. P. J. Ucko, R. Tringham, and
    G. W. Dimbleby, pp. 705-20. London: Duckworth & Co., Ltd.

---. Forthcoming. The contribution of Late Period studies to the
    social history of Ancient Egypt. In *Ancient Egypt: Prob-
    lems of history, sources and methods*, eds. D. O'Connor and
    D. Redford. Warminster, England: Aris & Phillips, Ltd.

Smith, P. E. L. 1968. New investigations in the late Pleistocene
    archaeology of the Kom Ombo Plain (Upper Egypt). *Quaternaria*
    9(1967):141-52.

Smith, P. E. L., and Young, T. C. 1972. The evolution of early
    agriculture and culture in greater Mesopotamia: A trial
    model. In *Population growth: Anthropological implications*,
    ed. B. Spooner, pp. 1-59. Cambridge: M.I.T. Press.

Sneh, A., and Weissbrod, T. 1973. Nile Delta: The defunct Pel-
    usiac branch identified. *Science* 180:59-61.

Sneh, A.; Weissbrod, T.; and Perath, I. 1975. Evidence for an
    ancient Egyptian frontier canal. *Am. Scientist* 63:542-48.

Soliman, S. M., and Faris, M. I. 1964. General geologic setting
    of the Nile Delta province and its evaluation for petroleum
    prospecting. In *Proceedings of the Fourth Arab Petroleum Con-*

gress (Beirut), vol. 23, pp. 1-11. Beirut: Arab Petroleum
Congress.

Spooner, Brian, ed. 1972. *Population growth: Anthropological
implications*. Cambridge: M.I.T. Press. 425 pp.

Steward, Julian. 1955. *Theory of culture change: The methodology of multilinear evolution*. Urbana: University of
Illinois Press. 244 pp.

Täckholm, Vivi, and Drar, M. 1950-54. Flora of Egypt: II and
III. *Bull. Fac. Sci. Fouad I Univ.* 28:1-547; 30:1.

Toussoun, Omar. 1925. Mémoire sur l'histoire du Nil. *Mem.
Inst. Egypte* 8-10:1-543.

---. 1932. Note sur les déserts de l'Egypte. *Bull. Inst. Egypte*
14:189-202.

Toynbee, A. J. 1935. *A study of history*. Vol. 1, rev. ed. London: Oxford University Press. 484 pp.

Trigger, B. G. 1965. History and settlement in Lower Nubia.
Yale Univ. Pub. Anthropol. 69:1-224.

---. 1968. *Beyond history: The methods of prehistory*. New
York: Holt, Rinehart & Winston, Inc. 105 pp.

---. 1970. The cultural ecology of Christian Nubia. In *Kunst
und Geschichte Nubiens in Christlicher Zeit*, pp. 346-79.
Recklinghausen, Germany: A. Bengers.

---. 1972. Determinants of urban growth in preindustrial societies. In *Man, settlement and urbanism*, eds. P. J. Ucko, R.
Tringham, and G. W. Dimbleby, pp. 575-600. London: Duckworth & Co., Ltd.

---. Forthcoming. Egypt and the comparative study of early civilizations. In *Ancient Egypt: Problems of history, sources
and methods*, eds. D. O'Connor and D. Redford. Warminster,
England: Aris & Phillips, Ltd.

Tringham, Ruth. 1972. Introduction: Settlement patterns and
urbanization. In *Man, settlement and urbanism*, eds. P. J.
Ucko, R. Tringham, and G. W. Dimbleby, pp. xix-xxviii. London: Duckworth & Co., Ltd.

Trochain, Jean. 1940. Contribution à l'étude de la végétation du
Sénégal. *Mem. Inst. Fr. Afrique Noire* 2:1-433.

Ucko, P. J., and Dimbleby, G. W., eds. 1969. *The domestication
and exploitation of plants and animals*. Chicago: Aldine
Pub. Co. 581 pp.

Ucko, P. J.; Tringham, R.; and Dimbleby, G. W., eds. 1972. *Man,
settlement and urbanism*. London: Duckworth & Co., Ltd. 979 pp.

Vandier, Jacques. 1936. *La famine dans l'Egypte ancienne.*
     Cairo: Institut Française d'Archéologie Orientale. 176 pp.
---. 1961. *Le Papyrus Jumilhac.* Paris: Centre National de la
     Recherche Scientifique. 349 pp.
Ventre, A. F. (Pacha). 1896. Crues modernes et crues anciennes
     du Nil. *Z. Ägypt. Sprache* 34:95-107.
Vermeersch, Pierre. 1970. L'Elkabien. *Chronique Egypte* 45:45-
     68.
Vignard, Edmond. 1923. Une nouvelle industrie lithique, le
     "Sébilien." *Bull. Inst. Fr. Archéol. Orientale* 22:1-76.
Vogliano, Achille. 1936. *Primo rapporto degli scavi . . . nella
     zona di Madinet Madi (1935).* Milan: Regia Universita di
     Milano. 88 pp.
Waddell, W. G. 1948. *Manetho.* London: Heinemann. 256 pp.
Weeks, K. R. 1972. The early dynastic palace. *J. Am. Res. Cent.
     Egypt* 9:29-33.
Wendorf, Fred, ed. 1968. *The prehistory of Nubia.* 2 vols.
     Dallas: Southern Methodist University Press. 1084 pp.
Wendorf, Fred, and Marks, A. E., eds. 1975. *Problems in prehis-
     tory: North Africa and the Levant.* Dallas: Southern Method-
     ist University Press. 462 pp.
Wendorf, Fred, and Said, R. 1967. Paleolithic remains in Up-
     per Egypt. *Nature* 215:244-47.
Wendorf, Fred, and Schild, R. 1975. The Paleolithic of the Lower
     Nile Valley. In *The Pleistocene prehistory of the southern
     and eastern Mediterranean Basin,* eds. F. Wendorf and A. E.
     Marks, pp. 127-70. Dallas: Southern Methodist University
     Press.
Wessely, Karl. 1904. Topographie des Faiyum (Arsinoites nomus)
     in griechischer Zeit. *Denkschr. Akad. Wiss. Phil. Hist. Kl.*
     50:1.
Westermann, W. L. 1919. The development of the irrigation system
     of Egypt. *Class. Philol.* 14:158-64.
White, L. A. 1948. Ikhnaton: The great man versus the culture
     process. *J. Am. Oriental Soc.* 68:91-114.
---. 1959. *The evolution of culture: The development of civili-
     zation to the fall of Rome.* New York: McGraw-Hill Book Co.
     378 pp.
Whiteman, A. J. 1971. *The geology of Sudan Republic.* Oxford:
     Clarendon Press. 258 pp.

Whittemore, T.   1926.   The excavations at el-Amarnah, season
    1924-5. *J. Egypt. Archaeol.* 12:3-12.

Whittle, E. H.   1975.   Thermoluminescent dating of Egyptian
    predynastic pottery from Hemanieh and Qurna-Tarif. *Archaeo-
    metry* 17:119-22.

Willcocks, William.   1889.   *Egyptian irrigation.* London: Spon,
    Ltd.   367 pp.

---.   1904.   *The Nile in 1904.* London: Spon, Ltd.   225 pp.

Willcocks, William, and Craig, J. I.   1913.   *Egyptian irrigation.*
    3rd ed.   2 vols.   London: Spon, Ltd.   884 pp.

Williams, M. A. J., and Adamson, D. A.   1974.   Late Pleistocene
    desiccation along the White Nile. *Nature* 248:584-86.

Wilson, J. A.   1955.   Buto and Hierakonpolis in the geography of
    Egypt. *J. Near East. Stud.* 14:209-36.

Winkler, H. A.   1938-39.   *Rock drawings of southern Upper Egypt.*
    2 vols.   London: Egyptian Exploration Fund.   44 + 40 pp.

Winlock, H. E.   1947.   *The rise and fall of the Middle Kingdom in
    Thebes.*   New York: Macmillan Inc.   174 pp.

Wittfogel, Karl.   1938.   Die Theorie der orientalischen Gesell-
    schaft. *Z. Sozialforsch.* 7:90-122.

---.   1957.   *Oriental despotism: A comparative study of total
    power.*   New Haven: Yale University Press.   556 pp.

Woenig, Franz.   1886.   *Die Pflanzen im alten Aegypten.*   Leipzig:
    Friedrich.   425 pp.

Yoyotte, Jean.   1959.   Nome.   In *Dictionnaire de la civilisation
    égyptienne,* ed. G. Posener, pp. 190-92.   Paris: Hazan.

---.   1973.   Réflexions sur la topographie et la toponymie de la
    région du Caire. *Bull. Soc. Fr. Égyptol.* 67:27-35.

Zeuner, F. E.   1963.   *A history of domesticated animals.*   Lon-
    don: Hutchinson Publishing Group, Ltd.   560 pp.

Zibelius, Karola.   1972.   Afrikanische Orts- und Völkernamen in
    hieroglyphischen und hieratischen Texten. *Beih. zum Tübinger
    Atlas Vorderen Orient* B-1:1-204.

Zohary, Daniel, and Hopf, M.   1973.   Domestication of pulses in the
    Old World. *Science* 182:887-94.

Zulueta, Julian de.   1973   Malaria and Mediterranean history.
    Parassitologia 15:1-15.